ALSO BY MARIANNE WILLIAMSON

Illuminated Prayers

The Healing of America/Healing the Soul of America

Emma and Mommy Talk to God

Illuminata

A Woman's Worth

A Return to Love

Enchanted Love

∽

The Mystical Power of Intimate Relationships

Marianne Williamson

SIMON & SCHUSTER

SIMON & SCHUSTER
Rockefeller Center
1230 Avenue of the Americas
New York, NY 10020

SIMON & SCHUSTER and colophon are registered trademarks of Simon & Schuster, Inc.

DESIGNED BY KATY RIEGEL

Manufactured in the United States of America

3   5   7   9   10   8   6   4   2

Library of Congress Cataloging-in-Publication Data
Williamson, Marianne, 1952–
Enchanted love : the mystical power of intimate relationships /
Marianne Williamson.
p.   cm.
1. Love.   2. Man-woman relationships.   3. Intimacy (Psychology)
I. Title.
BF575.L8W553   1999
299'.93—dc21   99-39531
CIP
ISBN 0-684-84219-X

Forget logic.

Forget your head.

Open your heart,

and come

with me.

❧

For you

Contents

INTRODUCTION
15

1.
The Enchanted Sea
21

2.
Of Space Captains and Angels
39

3.
Sacred Romance
51

4.

Sharing Our Gifts

75

5.

Love and Fire

101

6.

Grown-ups in Love

117

7.

Grace and Forgiveness

147

8.

Partnership

171

9.

Removing the Ghosts

191

10.

Ties That Bind

217

11.

Bodies and Soul

239

12.

When Form Changes

257

13.

Song of the Beloved

275

ACKNOWLEDGMENTS

283

Introduction

TRUE ROMANCE is not a situation so much as it is a realm of being, a realm unlike any other, permeating the air around us yet oddly invisible. It exudes a mystical power that calls to most of us once we are past a certain age. There is something there we want because we are human, and it clearly answers a basic human need.

True romance answers our need for adventure, for meaning, for magic, and for deep and soulful connection with another. It answers our spiritual as well as our emotional cravings. It is to grown-ups what the entire inventory of a toy store is to children. It makes our eyes grow large and bright the way theirs do when they have seen Santa Claus. In a very real sense, it *is* Santa Claus!

Yet romantic love is also like a train that cannot be ridden without a ticket. Some people have that ticket and some people do not. Some people have the emotional, psychological, and spiritual propensities for a truly romantic love, while others shy away from its deep and oceanic currents. Many, many people say they want it desperately, yet actually do everything in their power to avoid it.

This book is not about rules for intimacy. It is not about how to have a long-term relationship. It is not a formula. It is merely a woman's musings on what I have seen beyond the veil of love. It is about what I have come to recognize as the enchantment of a deep romantic encounter, which has less to do with quantity and more to do with quality, less to do with the outer world and more to do with inner domains. To have loved is like having traveled to a very distant and mystical land. This book is little more than impressions I have brought back from my journeys, but with this particular train ride, having been there is a ticket to going there again, and having truly understood someone else's journey can help convince the conductor that you belong on that train, and deserve a chance to ride it.

Most of the time, we fall in love but can't remain there. The world then calls the state we were in a delusion or infatuation. But we were not deluded. We were not just infatuated. We merely lacked, or someone else lacked, the emotional skills to hold on to the magic when the morning came. Later we would tell ourselves that that moment of magic had not been real, but that analysis is just a collective lie. We invented the lie as a way to face the disappointment of having been to the moon on a starlit night, and then fallen back down to what can seem like such a barren earth.

That lie is little more than a social conspiracy. It gives its adherents a perverse kind of comfort to think that our basic lack of courage is some form of psychological health. In truth, we can go to the moon and retain its magic for a lifetime. We can breathe in its spirit and never exhale. We can own the powers of romantic enchantment and experience all of life as a glistening adventure. We can enter the temple and receive a new heart, forever aglow with orange heat. Having gone to the moon, and believed in what we saw there, we can return with a ticket that will always take us back.

Forget your old ideas. Forget the lies they told you. Forget them all, and you will begin to remember. There is a realm of romantic enchantment that makes the world we are currently living in seem not so very important, and not even so very real.

That realm is entered two by two. It is not just an emotional vacation spot, but in fact our newest spiritual frontier. In fact, it is where we are supposed to live. And in that place, we do not just live. In that place, we live forever.

Oh Great Father/Mother God,

Please send my love to me.

From across the sea,

and over the mountain,

may he travel to my side.

And then, dear Lord,

when he arrives at my house,

may the food he finds here make him strong.

I await his coming.

I prepare my things.

Please ready my heart.

Amen

1

❧

The Enchanted Sea

I love the sea, the blue and the green and the wet and the cool. If I have to choose between the sea or you, I take you, but with sadness.

My favorite thing is to swim with you, to put the crown on my head and spray water in your face, to see you when you laugh like that, and pretend that I'm a little girl. I love to see that look on your face when you register that I'm not. . . . I know, I know, they always ask that, "Who are you, exactly?"

I just laugh and then I dive down deep, to find more pearls on the ocean floor. I will bring them back to you, my love. I will always bring them back to you. . . .

❧

I USED TO HAVE a thing about mermaids.

I felt I often met men who were lost at sea. I would meet them and lift them up, swim them home, and help them get their land legs back. But then I would have to go back into the ocean because I had only a fishtail. I envied the women with land legs, who got to greet these men upon their return and stay with them back on shore. I pitied myself all the lonely nights I spent swimming alone in a tempestuous sea, the stars above my only companions between rendezvous with drowning sailors.

When she was a very young child, I read *The Little Mermaid* to my daughter many times, and it was way too close to home. The mermaid Ariel got a different ending than I always did. At the end of the story she got to stay with Prince Eric in *his* world, and she didn't have to be a mermaid anymore. Something in me wanted that for myself. I would tell my Erics that I was going to do it their way, but then I found things so boring in their world. Yes, I wanted to be one of those land girls, but on another level I clearly didn't. I found I couldn't live without swimming, no matter how much I said otherwise. My tempestuous sea was a magical sea. And I didn't just *enjoy* the stars shining down on the ocean in the middle of the night; I finally realized I need them. If I had to choose between Eric and the sea, I was clearly more drawn to the sea. I saw that I wasn't made for Eric's world, and what I really wanted was a man who could swim without my help.

What I wanted was not a knight on a white horse. What I wanted was a knight on a dolphin, and ultimately that is what I found. For I learned some things about the Erics of the world. They are bored here, too. They want enchanted swims in the middle of the night, and are as open to the mermaid who swims them out to sea as to a mermaid who swims them back to land.

Forget *The Little Mermaid. Splash* is a better movie.

At the end of that one, the mermaid says to her love, "You know, I come from a much better place than this. There are just as many lights in my world and there is just as much excitement. There's as much going on down there as up here. In fact, in truth, it's a more civilized environment."

She had actually come, then, not just to be with him but to *retrieve* him. He flashed back to the moment when he'd met her. They had been children then, and their initial point of contact had not been earth, but sea. That was the point of their true and original connection, and its magic couldn't be exported to a sullied, weary, worldly environment. Enchantment is nontransferable. And so they both went back to sea. The mystic, and mystical lovers, learn this basic rule: Go where you're wanted. Go where you belong.

Mystical love, like mystical anything, exists in a different realm of consciousness than the one that dominates our daily lives. Emotional enchantment is conjured up, brought forth, and summoned from the underworld. It is not neurosis but mystical talent to know that and to know how to do it. In every woman, there is a latent priestess with the ability to invoke that realm. Mermaids are a kind of sexual muse, singing of a higher, more subtle, more magical dimension of life and love. In the enchanted romantic sea, we all have the power to heal and be healed. Our love, in that place, is a temple garden. Sex, in that place, is the door to the temple, and in that temple lies the power of God.

That sacred dimension of romance is what lovers long for now: the magical space of an enchanted intimacy. Many of us have been practicing its ways, unbeknownst to ourselves, for years. Some women have been practicing magic while others were doing housework. Some men have been practicing magic while others were practicing the worldly routines that rob their time and sap their life force. Some of us surrendered to the mystical waters that surround our earthly experience, and the surrender has at last turned out to be a blessing.

There was a time when the sea creatures landed on earth; now the creatures of the earth are heading back to sea. The enchanted lover—a candidate for mastery of both earth *and* sea—is rising up today in a creative swell. The reinvention of romantic love is our newest frontier, toward which our personal yearning is driving us in droves. There is another world beyond this one, which the mystically uninitiated simply cannot see. Their only response, were they to see a mermaid, would be to run some tests. Fishtails seem weird to them, but on the other hand, they don't see wings either.

In truth, they do not see at all. That is why they call love blind, for it is they who cannot see. There are some things that cannot be seen with earthly eyes.

Enchanted love is one of them. . . .

❧

If you will hold my hand, then I will hold my breath and cast my fate in the direction of my heart. I will put on hold my lesser dreams and reach for what is truly mine.

Say you will, and I will buy my ticket for this ride. It will not be cheap, nor always smooth. But I don't care. I don't care. I have finally come to that. . . .

~

OUR DEEPEST HUMAN NEED is not material at all: Our deepest need is to be *seen*. We need adventure. We need meaning. We need identity. We need love. Someone who has seen us through loving eyes has awakened us from the ranks of the formerly dead. Most people bear the terminal stress of walking the world unseen, a mere number or cog in a lifeless machine. Mystical romance is a space of resurrection and repair. It does more than help us survive a soulless world; it helps us to transform it.

The problem with most intimate relationships is that they are not romantic. They do not involve a deeper knowing, and thus there is diminished possibility of sacred, transformative sharing. To be truly seen, in all our innocence and glory, is to be truly healed. What we salute in one another, we call forth in one another.

So many people say that they are looking for love, yet they are actually committed to never finding it. Many people would really rather not know of the scars and triumphs of the person who lies in their arms. Many people who say they are looking for love are merely looking for superficial comfort. Real love entails readiness to die to who we were, in order to be born again prepared for love, truly worthy of the romantic heights. Real love is comforting, to be sure, but not always at first. In becoming romantic artists, we must pierce the armor that hides our hearts, and that piercing is not comfortable. It is horrible and painful. It can take years of tears to melt the hardness that develops in this world, covering our tender, gentler, inner selves. Tears for every devastating loss. Tears for every humiliating failure. Tears for every repeated mistake. Those who allow those tears, even honor those tears, are not failures at love but rather its true initiates. First the pain, and then the power. First the heart breaks and then it soars.

Love will push every button, try every faith, challenge every strength, trigger every weakness, mock every value, and then leave you there to die. But once you begin to turn the corner, to leave love's bush league and enter the pros, there is no worldly activity that can match the joy of flying like an eagle through the skies of a lover's heart.

഼഼

DO YOU REMEMBER when we were kids, reading about evolution? We were shown apes on the left side of a page, and a standing human being on the far right. That was how evolution was presented to us: as the rise of our species from ape to man.

But perhaps we should reconsider that picture. I think the standing human being belongs in the *center* of the page. Now, our arms are hanging down at our side, but what should happen next is that our arms move up slightly, in a position reminiscent of Jesus. It is a position that says simultaneously, "I am undefended" and "Come unto me." Can you imagine a picture of Jesus with his arms folded in front of him, striking a pose that suggests the attitude, "Don't even think about coming close to me"?

Our human arms will begin to lift, in a kind of Hallelujah posture, continuing to rise as a space on the back between the shoulder blades pops and our wings begin to sprout. At the far right of the page there will be a picture of an angel. For that is where we're headed now, as our evolutionary potential calls us to spring forward and become who we really are.

How will we get there? Quite simply, *with each other.* The highest purpose of intimacy is to call forth the beloved's soul.

Heaven is entered two-by-two. Enchanted intimacy is a temple of the Holy Spirit, where we are most quickly and most likely to be transformed by grace. We cannot remain who we used to be, once love has made it over our walls and begun to change our hearts.

The twentieth century is drawing to a close. We are exiting spiritual Dark Ages in which materialistic form and function were viewed as the primary reality of almost everything. Love hardly survived these times, though survive it did, in a fierce and miraculous way, often ravaged and torn by the mockery and denial of a loveless world. Magic was exiled to the margins of the mind, while true romance was diminished to the purview of fairy tales, and fairy tales, of course, were supposedly just for children. We applauded Romeo and Juliet, yet secretly supported the idiocy of their parents.

True romance had to go underground, as physical, then economic needs, took center stage. Women needed men to make their physical environment safe, to help protect the children and themselves. Nature needed both men and women to create more children, till the soil, and so on. But now the species has entered the next phase of our journey, the menopause of our existence, where our creativity will turn less physical and more spiritual. The planet needs more wisdom now, more than it needs more children. Men and women need each other, at least as much as we ever did, but for a deeper experience than mere procreation or protection. We need to partner in consciousness now, to conceive the miraculous things of spirit. Our most potent needs are psychological and emotional, our most potent language is poetry and myth, and our most potent love is forgiveness and compassion.

Our children, to survive, need this transformation in our experience of love. In order to protect them in ages past, we needed to be able to subdue our physical environment. Now, in order to protect the children, we must learn to pacify that same environment, to transform it from fear to love. Our relationships, at their highest, are conduits for a quantum leap forward. We need to be reborn as a human family now, for men and women to be made new, to be washed clean of the past that the world might start again. A soulful love is the psychic womb for new life, where our kisses have the power to transform us all.

೮೨

IT WAS MESSY when we were born into the body, and it is messy being reborn in spirit.

Growth is a detox process, as our weakest, darkest places are sucked up to the surface in order to be released. Often, upon seeing the weaknesses in each other, we have the tendency to go "Yuck!" and walk away on some level. But often it is not a change in partners but rather a change in perception that delivers us to the love we seek. When we shift our view of the purpose of intimacy—from serving our own needs as we define them to serving a larger process of healing—then an entirely new opportunity presents itself. Our wounds have been brought forward, not to block the experience of love, but to serve it. It is in the forgiveness of our weaknesses that we are healed of them, and the tenderness of a forgiven heart is a tenderness that will ultimately heal the world.

୧୨

You and I both know that we have shadow sides. We have edges, my darling, and resistances to love. If we're unevolved about this, then we will hurt each other, we will only cause pain. These aspects of ourselves could ruin this relationship. Let's consider this, before we embark.

In fact, we were brought together for healing purposes. There will be something in your personality which is bound to trigger the unhealed parts of me, and I will trigger yours.

But we can see this relationship differently. Through the grace of God, it can become a healing environment rather than an emotional torture chamber. Then I think I can work on those parts of myself, and you can work on those parts of you. We can even grow beyond these things. I just need you to know that I'm trying. Please share with me, but try not to attack or judge me for these wounds I carry. And I will try my best to do the same for you. Then holiness will be served here, and the relationship can deepen.

Forgive me, if you can, and I vow to try to forgive you.

❦

Can the purpose of a relationship be to trigger our wounds? In a way, yes, because that is how healing happens; darkness must be exposed before it can be transformed. The purpose of an intimate relationship is not that it be a place where we can hide from our weaknesses, but rather where we can safely let them go. It takes strength of character to truly delve into the mystery of an intimate relationship, because it takes the strength to endure a kind of psychic surgery, an emotional and psychological and even spiritual initiation into the higher Self. Only then can we know an enchantment that lasts.

We unconsciously seek the relationships that challenge us to deliver on our most soulful selves, as well as tempt us to fall into our most neurotic patterns. We must attend to the wound in order to heal it. That is the romantic Grail. It is what makes an intimate relationship so exciting, but also so difficult. Enchanted partnership begins with the conscious understanding, on the part of two people, that the purpose of their relationship is not so much material as spiritual, and the internal skills demanded by it are prodigious. High romance is not about past or future. It is not about practicality. It is not about society or worldly routines. It is an audacious ride to the center of what *is*, at the heart of every person. It is a bold and masterful inquiry into who two people really are and how we might become, while still on earth, the angels who reside within us.

ಲ

There is more to say, though we have not the language. There is more to see, though we have not the eyes. There is more to love, though we have not the heart. . . .

As yet, my love. As yet. For I believe in the power of love, and the magnetic draw of planets to their orbits. And you are drawn to encircle me as I am drawn to encircle you. Encircle each other we will forever, for our orbits are bound to one another's pull. The central sun has determined that, and its light, however dim or however bright, however central to our vision or merely peripheral and at times ignored, shall always call us back to our hearts. And back at home, in the haven of love, we will always find each other. I will be there, if only for a moment, and I will say to you, each and every time, "I remember, my darling. This is home to me."

"Do you think planets call each other 'Darling'?" you asked with a smile.

"On some level," I said, "I think they do."

ↄ

And that is where we all begin: a prince and princess longing for each other, wandering through foreign lands in search of one we lost. It is not an external "fix" we seek, but an internal blessing, and our souls will bend toward the possibility of union as surely as a flower bends toward sunlight. Wicked fairies and evil queens, monsters and dragons, and dangerous spells will always threaten our approach to heaven. Yet we are drawn to our destiny as if to a magnet, and while monsters can delay us, they have no power to change our destination. The map to our deliverance is held in trust and guarded by angels. We will encounter the darkness of a lonely existence, but find each other again in the light of an intense and compassionate understanding. We find in that place an unending kiss.

Each of us carries, etched on our hearts, instructions that read, "Come home. Come home." And the beloved arrives to take us there. Like the prince who comes to awaken Sleeping Beauty, he is an earthly prince who has received a higher Crown. With his Sword of Truth—his honesty and courage—and his Shield of Virtue—his integrity intact—he cuts through the brambles that surround the castle, and he frees us from the blackness of our too, too long night. Awakened, we embrace him, and together we enter enchanted realms. The kingdom of the heart is thus brought back to life, and life for everyone begins again.

Once upon a time, in a dimension of consciousness very far away, a mystical adventure began. Now, many ages later, we are beginning to awaken from our deep, deep sleep of separation and guilt. There is a sound of footsteps as the loved one approaches. He has made it to our side, and we are about to awaken from the deadness of our former selves. The beloved comes with an elixir of rebirth, in both hands, in every kiss, and our souls are reunited in God. We are free of our nightmares. We are forgiven and released. We are totally in love. We are so happy we are home.

Dear God,
I pray for the loves of my past,
those who chose me and those who did not.
I pray for their happiness,
their growth and their good.
May their hearts be filled with light
and their desires finally filled.
May they find what they are seeking,
although it could not be me.
Amen

2

❧

Of Space Captains and Angels

I came for you, I came for you, but you could not see me. I swam the seas, I traversed the coals, I died a thousand deaths for you. I found my way, I did, I did. But when I got there, you had fallen asleep. You had drunk their potions and I could not wake you.

I got there in time but your eyes were closed.

❧

OFTENTIMES, we pray for something and then miss the miracle when it actually happens. Many have said, "I wish I could have a great love," while blind to the fact that it was standing right in front of them. So often the issue is not learning how to attract love, but rather how to *recognize* love. Especially when we have waited so long, it is often an insidious trick of the mind to make sure we don't really see it even after it finally arrives.

Sometimes, love arrives as though it were a spaceship landing in the back yard. The captain comes out of the ship and says to us, "Hi, I'm here to beam you up! Come on! We're going!"

Yet so many times we reject him, saying, "Uh, well, I can't just *leave* here so fast. Actually, I can't even believe you're here. How long do I have to prepare my things?"

And he says, "You have no time at all. Your entire life has been spent preparing. Now, we must go quickly. If you wait, your eyes will adjust and you will no longer see me. I've just landed for a bit, to pick you up. You have an hour, max. You can make further plans from the ship."

The captain sees that we are bewildered, but so is he. "Haven't you been asking for this for years?" he asks.

"Well, yes," we say. "I have. But I guess I didn't think you were coming. . . . I sort of made a life for myself here, in the meantime."

"Not that much of one, judging from your prayers at

night," he tells us. "Let's go, if you're coming. I can't wait forever."

And then we say, if we say it, what is ultimately the most tragic thing we will ever say, and that is, "No, thank you."

No, I don't choose the ride, even though I want it desperately. No, I don't want to beam up now, even though it's a living hell down here. No, I do not choose the path of wild and radical and authentic love, even though I know I am dying without it. I think I'll just settle for "good enough."

And why do we do that? Why do we not receive with open arms the answers to our prayers? Because we ourselves are authoring what will one day look like natural selection. The human race is turning a corner, and those who choose not to make the turn will keep going straight until they fall off the cliff ahead.

Angels are onboard those spaceships, appearing everywhere now, often in the guise of loved ones holding the torch that would light our way through darkness. On the other side of that darkness is the light in which dreams come true. But there are demons in that darkness, to be sure, and we can feel them. They almost paralyze us with fear. All those unloved parts of ourselves are there, ugly and twisted and ready to destroy. They live in the darkness, on the other side of which is paradise itself. Even though the only way to paradise is through the darkness—and even though the fire of the angel's torch will burn the *demons* up, not us—we do not trust that. We lack faith. We are staunch and calcified in our refusal to choose love, and so we say to the angel, "No, you go ahead. I'll stay here."

The angel looks at us in disbelief; the refusal of ecstasy is unknown in heaven. The space captain can scarcely believe his ears, but noninterference in and respect for the choices of another human being is a must on the enlightened path. Not that you can force anyone onto a spaceship anyway. One only rides on the wings of an angel if one is seriously committed to the experience of heaven. The lure of hell is so very real here.

Still, as the ship takes off, the captain looks at the angel onboard and notices that there are tiny sparkling rivers of water, falling from her eyes.

Back at headquarters, the angel reports to higher-ups.

"He chose not to go."

The superior is silent, witnessing the angel's pain. The angel continues. "I can hardly believe it. He chose not to go."

"Do you think he understands the consequences?" asks the superior.

"I don't know," says the angel. "I think he thinks that staying there is the more responsible thing to do."

"Responsible . . . to whom? To what?"

"I don't know. It's strange. He's not ecstatically happy there, but he thinks it's his duty to stay. He feels it's an adult situation, and he lives in fear that he is not one."

"Yes, of course. Well, we've seen this before. They choose psychology over poetry. We keep trying to evacuate that realm before the storm hits, but people refuse evacuation."

"Yes."

"You prayed for him, of course."

"Oh, yes. With all my heart."

"Well. Job well done. Sorry if your heart was a little bruised on this mission. It's one of the risks, you know. It can happen, of course."

"Of course."

"Still, they're touching creatures. Contentious, but touching."

"Yes."

The angel was trained for love, she was disciplined in love, but her tears still flowed.

"You're excused. You may go."

As the angel turned around to weep, her superior called her

back. "I say, one thing. . . . Do remember—you'll see him again someday."

"Will I really, Master? Will I really?"

"Of course you will. You must cleave to your own faith at times like these. How else can you convince them of theirs, if you don't?"

❧

FOR MANY OF US, it's not that we don't want the spaceship to come get us, so much as we are completely taken aback by its form. We expect angels to have a different look. We don't recognize a gift from heaven, and how could we, when we have not truly believed that heaven exists? We don't quite compute what has occurred until often it's too late.

We didn't think this love would be human, with soft eyes and beautiful hands. We're thrown off by his profession, or her freckles, or his past. We didn't expect love to awaken our biggest fears and insecurities and doubts. We thought it would bring more immediate comfort. And so we wanted it, but we didn't. When you've lived in a dungeon for a very long time, the light, when you see it, actually hurts your eyes.

Jesus said, "Prepare, for when I come, I will come quickly."

The arrival of a soulful love often comes quickly, like that spaceship in the yard. There is little time to prepare before the flight takes off, just a window of opportunity, a cresting wave and then it's over. There will be little time to pack one's bags, so it is best to travel lightly through life. There will be little time to say good-byes, so it's best not to be living with people you know you should have said good-bye to long ago. We are living in the end times. New beginnings are upon us now.

We cannot burst through the old earth's atmosphere without another at our side. It takes two to make a spaceship. We can't generate the power to fuel the ship until we download the forces that only love can burn off. We must be fearless, as only love can make us fearless. We must be tender, as only love can make us tender. We must be fierce, as only love can make us fierce.

A man wrote to me once, "I don't think that the woman I am with can give me anything—what I am is what I allow myself to be when I am with her, or any one else for that matter. If we rely on externals for our power, strength, and influence, then we are powerless."

And since when is a *woman's love* an *external*? Did my friend learn this frightful delusion in a seminar somewhere, a factory for warmed-over platitudes that slightly honor human psychology, yet pay mere lip service to the power of true love? How weak we are when we are not yet ready to let love rip us open. Is this thought—that a woman's love cannot *transform* a man, that a man's love cannot *transform* a woman—really to be heralded as some kind of *wisdom*? It is not wisdom. It is a poisonous emotional pesticide that kills the fruits of love. It is a denial of the deeper regions of the heart, a resistance to the experience of freedom, an anguished, *"No, I cannot go"* when someone has said, "Come with me now. My love is the key to your prison door."

Such thinking, if not outgrown, is the deepest trap of all. It is not a repudiation of powerlessness, but a commitment to it. It is the cornerstone thought of a small and ultimately unlived life.

The miracle of love is expressed through other people. When a beloved is sent from God—and no one can tell you if they are, but the spirit within you—then they *do* hold the key to your soul's liberation. God has given it to them. They contain, in every touch and sigh, the information you need, the miraculous elixir to alchemize your weaknesses and turn them into strengths, to dry your tears and turn them into genius, to release your chains and set you free to be your passionate self at last. Woe to the one who does not yet know enough to say a deep and robust *"Yes"* to such love, to bow before its truth, to be humble before its power, to surrender to the gales of wind that storm through lovestruck hearts.

How tragic it is when we are too arrogant to defer to love, to put all small considerations aside and say, "I am going *there.*" How stupid it is to say no to the power of God's loving choice for us. How sad it is to think so little of ourselves that we cannot believe that he or she who stands before us, sent by God, is an angel come to give us wings. We have so little awe these days before the mysteries of the universe.

Yet if we are in the habit of denying God, then of course we deny His angels, too. And they hold, like pietas, the bodies of our unchosen loves. Angels weep—because their hearts are open—and I think God weeps as well to see such joy denied. And you continue to pray for what you've already received, and will one day realize that what you let fly by was a miracle intended to heal you. You might even say so, but by then it will probably be too late.

Angels do not light for long; they fly away when love denies them. They do not linger in the regions of earthly fear. Angels only come to pick up passengers, to fly away with them to paradise. Everything else is so ultimately silly, and everything else is so sad.

There is one more thing to know about the angel who came for you. The angel who came to fly you to paradise in reality had only one wing. She needed the angel in you to come forth, to be to her what she was willing to be to you. Thus your need for, your dance, your flight with each other. Together, you would have had one set of wings.

Next time she comes—whoever she is—perhaps you will not deny her. Next time she comes, be humble before the Lord. Next time she comes, admit your pain. Next time she comes, come forth yourself. Next time she comes, let go your resistance.

Next time she comes, be brave.

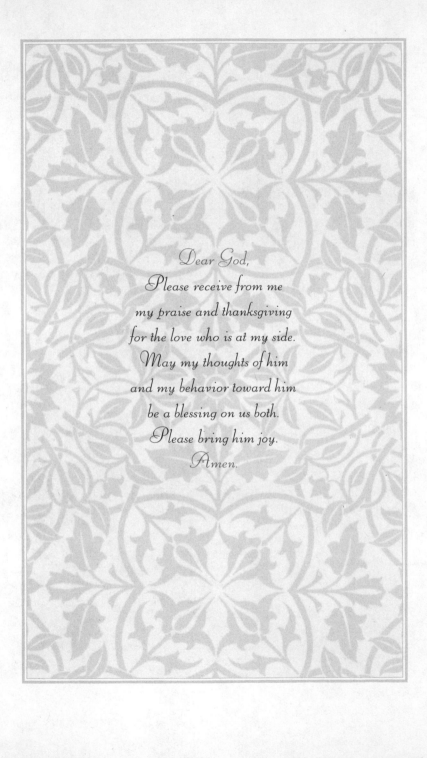

Dear God,
Please receive from me
my praise and thanksgiving
for the love who is at my side.
May my thoughts of him
and my behavior toward him
be a blessing on us both.
Please bring him joy.
Amen.

3

❧

Sacred Romance

And let me tell you of my happiness. I cannot not smile. I cannot be worried. I see meaning in all things.

They say this is not reality, that I am obsessed, that I am in denial. But they have no way of knowing how your ponytail delights me. And your hands. And your brain. And whatever else is part of you. . . .

❧

IS ENCHANTMENT just a metaphor? Is it merely an emotional state, something pink and fuzzy and

delicious perhaps, but nothing ultimately substantial or particularly real? The denial or invalidation of the power of enchantment is a block to our awareness of mystical domains.
We can only experience what we are willing to acknowledge.
There is no enchanted love in a nonenchanted world.

Some scholars believe that the Pyramids in Egypt were
built with the aid of sound. The power of sound, both posi-
tive and negative, is an underinvestigated phenomenon. Sound
techniques, including *chants*, might have been used by ancient
builders to break through the limitations of gravity. Some believe that through chanting an antigravitational forcefield was
created, making it possible to lift stones that would otherwise
have been too heavy to lift.

Firewalks, where people walk over red-hot coals without
burning their feet, are possible in part because many people
join together in chanting. Spontaneous enchantment occurs
in cases such as a parent's lifting a *car* to save a child pinned
beneath. There are realms in consciousness in which what we
think of as "normal" limitations—physical, psychological, or
emotional—simply do not apply. Enchantment is a power be-
longing to each of us, part of our birthright as children of
God. It is not an unnatural power but only an expansion of
what we now *consider* natural. A materialistic worldview is in-

vested in the notion of limits, and enchantment is a space of consciousness in which normal limitations disappear.

The word *enchantment* includes within itself the word *chant*. When we chant, our consciousness shifts into a different set of possibilities from the ones now defining our "normal" experience. When we fall in love—with a mate, a child, or even an idea—a spontaneous enchantment occurs, a blessing that is ours *for as long as we are capable of holding onto it*. We are bewitched, in those cases, and we are delighted.

Let's stay with those words: We are *bewitched* and we are *delighted*. The witch in each of us, our natural psychic powers, is simply, at those times, allowed to *be*. There is a suspension of the routine denial of magic that passes for realism in our modern, disenchanted world. The modern mind has been commandeered by alien mental forces, and they have dissuaded us of our magical powers. Today, at the end of the millennium, we are looking for the enchantment we threw away, many of us even suspecting that we cannot survive much longer without it. Told for centuries that enchanted power was merely the stuff of myth and fairy tales, now we are not so sure. Our strict adherence to rationalism has turned out to be less mental sophistication than collective gullibility, and we are ready to consider that what now passes for truth is in many ways fantasy, and what the world calls fantasy includes a lot of truth.

In *A Course in Miracles,* light is defined as "understanding." The world as we know it could not stand before the power of a human race that has remembered who we really are and reclaimed our spiritual powers. The investment in our forgetfulness, while in most cases unconscious, is enormous. That is why falling in love, when deep and masterful, is a powerful and revolutionary act. To be *delighted* is to be *awakened.* We have been asleep to our spiritual heritage for ages, and our greatest chance of awakening lies in awakening together.

Enchanted romance occurs not in the regions of our worldly thinking, but in another dimension: on the dark side of the moon. Some things are seen more clearly in light, and some things are seen more clearly in darkness. The word *occult* means "hidden." Something hidden, in a psychological sense, is not negative but merely mysterious, neither seen by the physical eye nor obvious to the rational mind. God hath made both day and night. What is hidden during the day is often magical at night. The dark side of the moon is still a part of the moon.

If we want enchantment in our daily lives, we must cultivate its spiritual conditions. We must learn to give and to receive, to appreciate joy and give it to others, to see the magic in ordinary things, and seize the moment like the key to love that it is. Most people, when they first fall in love, are willing enough to fly, to be poetic, to grab the golden ring of infinite possibility. Yet how quickly then, having thus expanded, they constrict again to fit the littleness of the disenchanted world. They prefer dry prose to poetry, and dry prose is death to love. Back on earth after a flight through the sky, the coward at love chooses not to rock the boat of practicality and routine. Little does the coward know that the boat itself is sinking.

The dark side of the moon is not the enemy of sunlight but its esoteric twin. It is the dance floor of an illumined mind. Psychological analysis can never quite pin down its power (Goethe once said, "To analyze is to murder"), for it evades the arrogance of the conscious mind. With our rational understanding we can fly a man to the moon, but getting love to fly can be a harder job. It doesn't respond to our ego-based assumptions, and there is no scientific formula that can conjure it up or make it soar. Love is a mystery that cannot be approached through will; it responds most generously to humbled souls. In some unexplainable way, it seems to grace us when it's ready. Our greatest tool for bringing love into our lives is to pray, "Dear God, please prepare me. Open me up and make me new. Destroy the walls that surround my heart."

✧

I don't know if we can hold onto this, you said.

Why couldn't we? I asked. I could see you slipping back, and it scared me.

We can't be this way, and pay the bills. We can't be this way, and stay responsible. We can't be this way, and . . . I don't know. I just don't think we can be this way.

Then you can't. But I can.

And then I swam away. . . .

✧

Romance is one of the sacred temples that dot the landscape of a human life. It is transformative and healing when approached with reverence, but always potentially dangerous when approached with anything less. We tend to lack humility toward love, to patronize it rather than bow before it, to put mundane considerations before the emotional need to hold someone in our arms. And then we complain because life is so boring. What a price most of us have already paid for our shallowness in the face of love.

Like a castle surrounded by a deep, impenetrable forest, an enchanted love is as forbidding as it is inviting. The forest is full of magical dragons that assault the casual passerby. Not just anybody gets to stroll through the castle gates, play around inside the courtyard, and get out of there alive. It takes a prince to make his way through the forest and deal with all those dragons. Then, even if he has the *cojones* to do that, he needs to find the sleeping princess and kiss her so perfectly that she actually wakes up. That he can only do if his sword and shield are with him. Otherwise, the dragons of love will chew him up and spit him out, and the princess will grieve that, one more time, someone tried but could not rescue her.

That is where most of us—princes and princesses alike— usually are, when we wander into the therapist's office or support group, looking for comfort after doing some time in the battlefields of love. Millions of us, like naïve soldiers singing songs at the beginning of a war, thinking this was going to be an easy enough time and then coming home in body bags— that is our psychic history of love. We then sit at the feet of friends and counselors, weeping and moaning, what did I do wrong? No one had told us we needed a sword. No one mentioned we would need a shield. And no one had taught us the mystical basics. We hadn't really known that there *were* any.

Love is a hero's journey, and the hero's journey is a noble but difficult path. Recognizing this, and honoring it as such, endows romantic love with the grandeur and power it deserves. An overly casual mind might attract love easily enough, but lacks the emotional musculature necessary to maintain it. Love is a daytime as well as a nighttime activity, and it demands that we become creatures of both. Every part of who we are is brought up for review, that we might let go what is heavy and low within us, and claim what is light and high. Romance then becomes a spiritual missile, taking us from where we've been to where we need to go.

Where have we been? In darkness. Where are we going? To the land of the sun. Intimacy reaches now for its sacred element, bringing hearts together to form forcefields of light bright enough to cast out the darkness of the world. The entire human race is now crossing from one realm into another, and relationship is one of our modes of crossing, carrying us across the waters of consciousness to the land that lies beyond.

There is no way to make that journey without divine illumination to light our way. There is a holy relevance to love's deeper enchantments, giving meaning to its joy and also to its pain. Sacred understanding holds our hearts together, supporting us as we support each other in climbing the stairs to our higher selves. It is our medicine when the heart is breaking, feeling that the labor we are in, trying to birth our own souls, is far too hard and we will die if we go on. Invisible forces minister to us during our transfiguration from self to Self. Love comes to slay what needs to be slain in us, in order for something new to emerge. It is hard to go through this, to surrender deeply to the waters of intimate romance, to wield its power and endure its pain, without a sense of God's love moving through us in the process.

God gives us new eyes, new ears, new hearts, and new minds. And we need them if we are to learn to truly love. The body's eyes show us wonderful things, from paintings to bodies to children to nature. But they are also vulnerable to the tricks of maya, the ghostly dance which makes up the kaleidoscope of the physical world. Another world, to which God delivers us, awaits us on the other side of our illusions. Enchanted love will take us there.

When love is fun, it is sublime. When it hurts, it is excruciating. When it is true, it is enduring. When it is enchanted, it is miraculous. That realm is now beckoning the entire world, and enchanted lovers, with a newly wise and innocent look in their eyes, are both heralding its existence and announcing its address.

❧

Your eyes are like street lamps to me. They tell me I am home, this is where I live, I am safe here, I have made it. There is someone waiting here to talk to me and hold me. . . . I want to know everything, and I am rushing now across the grass, to throw open the door, to say "I'm home!", to see your eyes, to know that this is the right address, the right address at last, thank God.

❧

Romance is an emotional and sexual shadow dance, performed by our truer selves behind a spiritual veil. This veil is not illusion but a gossamer reality. Within that reality we are all afloat in a liquid amniotic spirit, preparing to be born anew.

The art of love is an emotional midwifery. We hold each other as we emerge together into the light of a new life, both exhilarating and terrifying. The monster can get very loud within us, as the rattle of death overtakes it. Just at the point where the beast is about to turn into beauty, a cowardly, uninitiated partner might say, "This is too high maintenance. I can't do this. I'm leaving."

We find a whole new dimension of "for better or for worse." The light of love is bound to shine on the creepy, crawly aspects of ourselves, those pieces of former brokenness lying hidden beneath the rocks within. Inside the tomb lie our dormant energies, our passion and our love, seemingly dead but only sleeping; love is come to remove the rock, heralding the resurrection of sanity and Self.

The first one to see the resurrected Jesus on the road was Mary Magdalene. Her eyes were the most attuned of anyone's to the sight of His luminous Self. Not his mother. Not his disciples. Not his followers. *Her.* She saw him first because she was in love with him. Indeed, some believe she was his wife. For two thousand years, their story has been psychically sealed, our collective mind not yet ready to behold the mystery of their divine connection. Yet as our romantic consciousness rises, illumined and blessed at a whole new level, their union will become more clear. Who he was to her, and who she was to him, is one of the cosmic hieroglyphs still locked within the soul.

Pieces of their mystery are now becoming clear, as one letter is decoded, then another follows quickly. We are beginning to understand the word *Behold*. Jesus and Magdalene *beheld* each other. There is no true *being* without *holding*. Until we have learned to hold each other, we haven't truly learned to be.

To say, "I behold your beauty (or your strength, or your courage, or whatever)" means, "I know that your beauty is there, because I see it even if you don't yet see it yourself. You are safe to bring it forth in my presence, and when you do, I will hold it like a precious gift. I will receive it with love and honor." It is not enough for me to see something in you; I must learn to *hold* what I see. Until we are blessed by the mystic's love, we wander forever in the living death of our woundedness and pain. Then, in an enchanted moment, we are free of who we used to be: the be-loved be-holds us, and death turns into new life.

❦

They were wicked to me. I know they were. They wanted to kill me. I know they did. They think I'm bad. I know they do.

And you—your eyes are even harder to bear. Do you pity me?
No. Do you laugh at me? No. Do you scoff at me? No.
I looked at you.
Now relax, you said. The past is over, and it was just a dream.
My love is here with you, and my arms are the door. Just be with me
now. There is nothing else.

❧

From ancient Egypt, there emerged one of the greatest love stories in the world: the romance between the goddess Isis and her brother Osiris. When their wicked brother Seth killed Osiris in a jealous rage, Isis drew upon her mystical power, the strength of her divine love, to bring Osiris back from the dead. That is the power inherent in love: to awaken the beloved from the state of the psychically dead. On the night of their re-union, celebrating the resurrection of their romance, Isis and Osiris made love and conceived a wondrous child.

Seth, as one would imagine, went bonkers. "Now," he thought, "I must kill Osiris again, yet this time I will chop him up into many pieces, so that my sister will never be able to put him back together again."

Then Seth murdered Osiris again, this time dismembering

him and scattering the pieces of his brother's body throughout the various regions of Egypt. Only Osiris' penis (it's interesting to note) went elsewhere, swallowed by an alligator and sunk to the bottom of the Nile.

Time fulfilled itself and Isis gave birth, now holding in her arms the divine child Horus. Seth, still on a rampage, sought to kill them both. Worried that their traveling together made the child an easier target, Isis sought a surrogate mother to take care of her son. Yet not just any woman would do: only a Goddess could provide divine milk with which to suckle a holy child.

So it was that Isis sought out the Goddess Hathor, begging her to take the baby Horus and raise him as her own. Visually, Hathor would forevermore be pictured as a woman with a cow's ears, the Goddess who provided mother's milk to the divine baby Horus.

And something very interesting happened when Horus grew into manhood, in a drama quite different from what the Western mind is used to. When he matured, Horus did not separate from Hathor. He did not seek another woman for his bride. Rather, Hathor herself *transformed.* Having acted as his mother, she now became his wife. *She was the same woman, honored for the various parts of herself.* No split between Mary and Magdalene here, no mother and whore dichotomy, no shameful introduction of guilt onto sex, or onto women. The Goddess retained all her many faces, from maternal to erotic to divine. Neither Goddess self nor sexual self nor mother self were diminished by the presence of the others.

The Egyptian temple of Hathor is, for me as a woman, the most powerful sacred site in the world. We find the force of Hathor there in her vast feminine glory, resplendent in her power to raise up both men and women from the depths of our brokenness and littleness and shame. There have been women in the modern age who reflected Hathor's magic. Jacqueline Onassis and Princess Diana both come to mind, their motherhood and sexuality not opposed, but playing off each other like the colors in mother-of-pearl. Neither one de-sexed herself in order to be a "good mother," nor did she ever play down her motherhood in order to remain an object of sexual glamour. Both fused the two so easily that one has to remind oneself that, before them, motherhood had come to mean, for generations of American women at least, less sexy hair, less sexy clothes, less sexy self. And, in addition to sexual glamour and an almost fierce devotion to their children, both women held almost an other-worldly sway over the hearts and minds of millions.

Hathor did not have to make a choice between essential aspects of her total self, and neither should mere mortals. For none of us *are* mere mortals. The gods and goddesses are alive in all of us, to the extent to which we are alive in them.

Sex, mysticism, and motherhood form a feminine trinity. A trinity represents mystical union among three pieces of the universe that should not be kept apart. In both men and women, the separation of essential aspects of our humanity is the cornerstone of the fallen self, the pieces of the murdered Osiris new strewn throughout the land. There could hardly be a more dramatic image of the separation of sex from self than the swallowing of a man's penis by an alligator! Osiris was literally dismembered, his penis not even remaining aboveground, but rather sunk to muddy depths at the bottom of the subconscious mind. And does it not remain there to this day?

Then you and I, adult children of a spiritually barbaric century, come breezing along, looking for love and expecting it to be easy. Ha! Nothing misunderstood is easy. Nothing that is not naked blesses. Nothing superficial heals.

Isis and Osiris and Horus—and Seth as well, I'm afraid—all live within us. The feminine in each of us is Isis, breathing love into her deadened other half. The masculine in each of us is Osiris, noble and brave, yet torn apart by attacks from a jealous world. The fear-based ego in each of us is Seth, set out to destroy the experience of powerful, total, authentic love. The highest potential in each of us is Horus, set to reclaim humanity's divine identity, suckled by a divine mother, married to a divine Goddess, first pharaoh in the psychic land of the Gods.

It is the role of Horus to "re-member" his father—to bring back together the pieces of the lost and broken god-self within us. Horus is the fully actualized self, born of divine parents, living a life of unity and integrity, here to rule and harmonize the forces of the universe. At every stage of his life, there is a woman there to support and nourish him, and he has no problem letting one woman play all the parts.

In sacred temples throughout Egypt, priceless sculpture and painting created by ancient artisans in honor of their gods were viciously defaced by early Christians. All visual representations of a God other than Jesus Christ were deemed sacrilegious, to be violently hacked away by fanatical Coptics during the early centuries of the first millennium. But nowhere is the hacking more brutal or more vicious than at the Temple of Hathor. She was barely allowed to remain within her temple space at all. Her defacement there is so pronounced, so anti-woman, so violently destructive of any feminine aspect of God, that any sensitive person approaching this place is automatically plunged into the horror of female crucifixion. That crucifixion has been continuous— from Hathor's Temple to medieval witch-burnings to the emotional wounds within us still. We are crucified not by men but by spiritual ignorance. It is an ignorance borne of outright terror of the forces of love on the dark side of the moon.

֍

But wait, I said. How do I know that if I go with you, I will be okay, and I'll function, and I'll survive?

Have you ever stopped to ask yourself what kind of life you are surviving? Have you thought about the kind of journey I am asking you to take with me? Would you really rather stay here in the land of the dying and call it life?

No, no, no, you just found me at a low point. I had best go back to where I knew what to do. Thanks for saving me, but now that I'm saved, I think that I had best go back.

And so I did, and now I look for you, but all I can find are your eyes in the sky, on certain days, under certain conditions, and while they do not reproach me, they seem to miss me as much as I miss you.

ev

Now, at the dawn of the twenty-first century, the Goddess rises up to resurrect the deadened soul of modern consciousness. Romance is one of her wombs, as breathing life into a destroyed beloved is very much her specialty. There is an eternal temple dance, a romantic *ballet deux* of hearts, where day after day, night after night, in every corner of the world, Osiris longs to receive new life and Isis longs to give it. In the middle of war, in the midst of suffering, on our marriage beds and even on our deathbeds, we reach for each other and say, "I love you so much."

This is so much more than sex on vacation, a night to remember, or a power struggle between romantic partners. Sacred romance is a call of the soul, a bid for life in spite of it all. It is nothing less than an assignment from God. "I have chosen someone to heal you," He says, "and I have chosen someone for you to heal. Enter the temple and expose your wounds. Be not afraid. My spirit will heal both of you. Together you shall receive new life."

೭ಾ

Come down, you said, to the river with me. I want to bathe you in what I know.

And then you will never cry again. You will see where your dreams are only dreams, and we will visit together the land of the awake. I will give you a diamond to wear on your heart, and it will shine in you forever. I will give you a kiss that will stay in your mouth, and the more you speak, the more it will bless.

You will be a goddess then. For thousands of years they will proclaim your name. Throughout the ages, they will know of you that you lifted me up when I was dead, and thought my death an unalterable state. You breathed new life into my mind, for only you were sane enough to think that such was possible. In return I gave my heart to you, and behold, we both now live.

From this point forward there is a new horizon. If any man or any woman ever sink below the line, if they cannot breathe or they cannot reach, they will only have to call our names. And the power of our love will reach to them. We will lift them up and make them one, as you and I are one this night. Cling to me, as I cling to you. Together we will glue together the broken pieces of the errant world. Forever we will live like this.

Forever we will live. . . .

Dear God,

May the man I am with
emerge into his greatness.
May the woman I am with
emerge into her glory and her joy.
May we leave behind
our broken selves,
and emerge into the light.
Heal our wounds
and bless our dreams.
Thank you, God.
Amen

4

❧

Sharing Our Gifts

My darling, go home and tell your mother that you are coming with me. Tell her she needs to pack for you, for where we are going it can get quite cold.

Now go and be swift, for we must not tarry. The hour is late, and our dreams are waiting.

I hold your dreams very close to my heart, and I hope that you hold mine.

❧

THE MORTAL MIND focuses on the physical; divine mind focuses on the spiritual. The mortal mind believes in limits; divine mind believes in limitlessness. The mortal mind believes in guilt and error; divine mind believes in forgiveness and innocence. Which mind we choose to think with literally makes the difference between relationship heaven and relationship hell.

The mortal mind asks, "What am I getting here?" Divine mind asks, "What am I giving here?" The mortal mind says, "Why isn't the relationship this or that?" Divine mind asks, "What is the gift here? What is the meaning of this love?" The mortal mind says, "So-and-so did this wrong, or that wrong." Divine mind says, "I desire to focus on the light in others, that I might experience the light in myself."

Believing in finite resources, the mortal mind guides us to selfish thought and selfish behavior. This in turn destroys relationships.

In fact, it is divine mind which illumines our path to true intimacy, guiding us to the thoughts and feelings and perceptions that genuinely join our hearts to the hearts of others. For one thing, it makes us givers and not takers, and we only get to keep what we give away. Love guides us toward the spiritual and emotional generosity without which there is no true depth of connection, mystical or otherwise.

❧

I WAS WORKING once with a group of teenagers, all of us sitting together in a small circle. I led an exercise in which we were to go around the group, each sharing our deepest dreams. Then, after each person had shared his or her dream, everyone else in the circle was to actively support it. At the beginning of the exercise, it went like this: Michael said that his deepest dream was to be a great artist. I then asked Shelly to support that dream, and she looked not at Michael but at me, and said, "Yeah, I think Michael could be a great artist. He draws real well."

I said, "No, Shelly, look right at Michael. Look into his eyes. Speak to him in first person. Tell him if you think he has talent, and tell him you think he will be a great artist someday."

"Michael," she said, looking at him but still averting her eyes, "I think you're a real good artist. I think you'll be one, one day."

"Not quite enough, Shelly," I said. "It's your job to *convince* him. Helping someone feel confident is part of holding their dream."

"Michael," she said, "I am absolutely sure that you will be a great artist someday. Your pictures are fantastic. I love them. One day the entire world will love them."

"Much better, Shelly," I said. "But life is hard, and he probably still needs a little more fortification. Why should he believe you?"

"Believe what I'm telling you, Michael," she said, now looking into his eyes as though the knack had been there all along. "Because I know what I know. I know this is true."

"Shelly," I said. "Where is Michael's dream?"

"It's in his heart," she said, looking at me.

"Where else is his dream now, Shelly?" I asked her. "Is it anywhere else?"

"I guess it's in my heart," she said.

"Then tell *him* that."

"I'm holding your dream in my heart, Michael." Her smile was ageless now, and she held his gaze.

"Tell him it will be safe there, Shelly."

"It will be safe there. I will keep it for you," she said. "You don't have to worry. I'm your friend and I'm holding your dream."

I looked over at Michael and he was crying. I almost cried

too, thinking how much pain I went through before I knew how to hold a man's dreams.

❧

YET IT'S HARD to show up for someone else when you don't yet know how to show up for yourself. How can you give of yourself when you don't really think you're anything worth giving? How can you extend your light when you don't really believe there is any in you? But the light in us is the light of God, and it's there because He put it there. Lack of self-esteem is more arrogant than it is humble, suggesting the idea that God somehow created junk.

Low self-esteem is delusional. We're all one in spirit, and thus we are deeply equal in essence. It is our spiritual essence and equality, not our differences, that form the basis for true self-esteem as well as regard for others. We all just happen to be hosts to God. So what's not to love?

What this means, among other things, is that all of us have a lot to give. In fact, we have not yet begun to scratch the surface of our infinite potential. All of us are faucets through which divine waters would flow forth freely. And God's gifts would not only pour into us every moment but would also pour *through* us, seeking to cleanse and nourish the entire world. We block that flow when we think that we personally have nothing to give. It's the water, not the faucet, that ultimately matters. In any moment that our desire and willingness is to be of service to another, the faucet is miraculously turned on. If our prayer is, "Dear God, please use me to be of service," then that is what we will be. And it is not for us to judge either the size or value of our gifts. Our job is to try to get out of the way, to defer to the spirit moving within us and become open channels for the flow of God's love. That is what Jesus meant when he told us to become like little children: There is an innocence and grace that naturally and automatically pull all things into harmony and balance. Finding that place, through prayerfulness and meditation and constant practice, delivers us to an energy more peaceful, more illumined, than the ego mind can even conceive of. That energy lives by its own dictates, and would have us do the same. We are literally guided by its light, effortlessly, to higher and higher paths of unfoldment. When we step back and let a higher power lead us, what emerges are plans and schemes that far surpass the little ideas of our mortal minds.

A man once said to me, "But what would a day with us

look like?" I could not answer him in a way that could satisfy his then-current frame of reference. What love does, if it is allowed to, is to combine people's energies in ways that lift their lives to a mode of divine right order, where new ideas, new possibilities, and new opportunities for growth emanate directly from the heart of God.

Our job is to not abort the process.

I was having lunch one day with a very successful friend who was visiting my town. I said, "What are you doing tonight?" He said, *"Nada,"* with a tone that implied, "I'd love to do something!"

"Well," I said. "There's a woman speaking on relationships tonight over at the church. She's really good. Do you want to come?"

"Great!" he said.

About an hour later, I had seen more of his life. It is a very big life on external levels. As the day wore on, I began to lose faith in the adequacy of my gift to him.

Finally I said to him, "You know, I don't mean to disinvite you, but I really don't know if you would like this talk. I'm not sure. . . . I mean, I don't know. . . . Although, I could have someone pick you up, of course. . . . I couldn't take you, but someone else could pick you up, and you could leave when you want to, and I mean, well, I would have you sit next to me, but then you could leave. . . ."

Blah, blah, blah, blah, blah.

He of course opted for dinner and a movie with his friends, and I went to the lecture at the church. The entire talk related to the very issues that my friend was dealing with in his life. It would have delighted him. I had denied him the gifts that were trying to find him, by diminishing my own.

The next night I saw him and said, "I should have kidnapped you last night and taken you to that talk."

"I know," he said. "I could feel that."

I learned something from that experience. My temporary lack of self-esteem in relation to the grand level of my friend's existence had blocked the truth from me: that all gifts are equally significant, because they have nothing to do with the material world. I do not serve the world by false humility. I serve the world most by humbly accepting that God uses me, because God uses everyone and everything to serve the process of universal healing. We are constantly offered the gifts we most need to receive. The way to receive our gifts is to give our gifts, and that we cannot do if we are always questioning this value.

There is an overall scheme of perfection in the universe, and thinking we are somehow not part of its design only interferes with its unfoldment.

❧

THE CHALLENGE of our generation is to move from *me* to *we.* That is the maturity we assume when we wish to learn to love each other from a healed and holy place. Narcissistic people are lonely.

Narcissistic people misunderstand independence, often mistaking the commitment to aloneness for psychological health. A woman I know once told me she was deeply touched by a man she had just met, who lived in another town. While they hadn't known each other for long, she felt in her heart that something very special had occurred between them, a romantic magic that was very rare in both their lives.

Seeing her a couple of weeks later, I asked her how her relationship was going. "Well, it's not," she told me. "I mean, after all, I just met him. I think he's fabulous, and we lift each other up into some incredible place. But I can't go making major life decisions based on *that*."

I hesitated. "Whoa," I said. "I could have sworn we could. Should we base life decisions on something less important?"

She gave me the following excuses for why she couldn't be with this man: one, he lived in another town (as though there aren't airplanes); two, another man might be moving to be with her in this one (although she said she wasn't in love with him); and three, she didn't know if she could be with this new love and still pursue her career. What I kept thinking, as I listened to her, was that this was a woman who was unwilling to *reach* for love.

She was like someone waking up in the morning and on her bed is a breakfast tray, the morning paper, a good book, a telephone, and a remote for the TV. It's all there. She'll reach over for something to do, at some point, when she happens to be in the mood to do so.

So romance with this man was simply that for her: something else lying around, like a newspaper or a book that she might pick up sometime. She might reach over, but she had no plans to reach *for*. Neither her society nor her life experience had taught her that love is infinitely more important than either a breakfast tray, telephone, newspaper, book, or TV. Her heart told her it was—I could tell that from the way she described her feelings—but modern culture had told her, if anything, how neurotic her heart was to want to jump at this, how much more important a career is than passionate love, and how serious and adult it is to honor material considerations over the love we feel inside. She hadn't yet considered that the voice of the heart is the voice for God.

She hesitantly asked me what I thought.

"I'm not sure you want to know," I responded.

"But I really do want to know—sort of," she laughed.

I paused, and then I said, "I think you're dishonoring yourself. Jobs, houses, money, and even sex come and go, but love is like some magical bird. And once it flies away you have absolutely no power over if or when it will ever return."

"It surprises me to hear you say that," she said softly. "You're a career woman. You obviously put your career first."

"Boy, is that not true," I said. "It might look that way to you, but I think that if I put my career first in the way you mean that, it wouldn't be much of one. When my heart talks, I try to listen. Why should I validate my heart in every other subject, but not relationships? I don't think there's any less importance in loving a man than in loving anything else. Relationships are certainly part of God's plan! And everything in life is better when we have love in our lives."

I had been like that woman once, thinking romance and

God lived in different corners of the universe. Yet it was all just an insidious effort of my mind to keep my relationships out of God's hands.

I thought my romantic longings deserved less respect than my longing for professional achievement. Many women of my age grew up with the twisted idea that men and babies should be secondary goals. What's true love and the miracle of giving birth, next to the awesome high of delivering your first quarterly report?

That's how dumb we were.

We were taught to go after things that we could control. Love, of course, drives *you*, and not the other way around. Most of us, both men and women, are terrified of merging our hearts with another. We say we're not, but we are. Even when we're in relationships, we avoid their mystical power. We turn lovers into roommates, butlers, or maids. We avoid the real light at the center of romantic passion. We're afraid it would swallow us up.

And that's because it *would*, and it *does!* Overwhelming our sense of separateness is in fact love's spiritual purpose. The alchemy of love turns the small into the infinite. Enchanted romance is a fire meant to burn up our sense of otherness, from other people and from God Himself. So many of us went around saying for years, "I lose myself in other people too much. I need to stay out of relationships." And often that was true. But after a period of time, that thought just became a rationalization for the avoidance of love. The day came, once we had developed ourselves and knew who we were, when many of us were only too happy to give up the trappings of our separateness. To resist intimacy, out of fear that if you love you will risk codependency or enmeshment, is like resisting eating food out of fear of obesity. That, as we know, is not wisdom but severe dysfunction. At a certain point, once you've established your separate identity, it's imperative that you let yourself lose it again. Otherwise, you can never know love.

❧

Dear God
I feel that if I love this person,
I could lose everything that I have.
I have no idea where this love might take me,
and in his presence,
I don't even care.

Is it strength, or weakness,
to have faith in this feeling?
Illumine my mind and heart,
dear God,
for my ship is lost at sea.
Amen

❧

A career, you can control. Love, you can't. Terrifying news that, but wonderful once you get the hang of it.

The reason intimacy is so important is that it *does* force us to surrender our sense of separateness, not in a neurotic way but in an enlightened way. I understand why women had to completely renegotiate our terms of partnership, after centuries of institutionalized subjugation, but at a certain point we have to show up enough to at least give men a chance to do it right. Both men and women are trying very hard today to rethink, redefine, and recast romantic partnership.

What I used to think—what lots of women I know used to think—is that I had more important things to do than love a man. To me, surrender to a man meant that I would have to give up myself so he could shine. I know there are men in relationships with whom that would indeed be true, but their numbers are diminishing. There's a whole new world now, with new possibilities for union and equality.

Everyone, whether men, women, or children, as individuals or collectively, follow cycles of growth and rhythms of becoming. Whether a phase represents physical growth, as in a child's body, or the awareness of an entire species, there is an evolutionary imperative to keep moving in the direction of a higher good.

The times we live in are like a planetary menopause, with hormones and chaos and longing leaking out all over. "I'm not who I used to be, but who am I then?" is practically painted in red over every event. And every unit of human identity—every one among us—is struggling to find the answer.

Women have been struggling to emerge like butterflies from the cocoon into which we were forced for the last few thousand years. The journey of our self-actualization—of our rising from the ashes of past physical, mental, and emotional oppression—is clearly one of the major dramas of modern Western civilization. The emergence of true feminine power and glory, while not easy and perhaps rarely accomplished in full, is at least a conscious effort on the part of millions of women.

But starving people have a hard time sharing food. When we ourselves are needy, the needs of others will always come last. So perhaps it's not an accident that women, having been starved for so long and now finally experiencing how it feels to be at least partially fed, are beginning to notice the emotionally starving men all around us. They are starving, among other things, for our attention and approval. Isis didn't say to Osiris, "Just stay down there! I don't care." Men, like women, have the need to be *called forth*.

It's understandable that women's adoration was withheld from our men for a while; we had thousands of years of bottled-up rage to express, and it didn't exactly put us in a demure mood while we were going through that. Yet now, there is a new coming together between the sexes, as we find ourselves at a higher level of mutual honor and need. "I can't go any further without you," is at first a feeling we are afraid to admit, but then we exult in saying it once we know we're in a place where it's safe to do so. At a certain point, a woman can't conceive new life, whether her own or her child's, without a man's input, and neither can he reproduce without us. Nature has ordained our utter interdependence, which is not, when seen through enchanted eyes, our damnation but our salvation.

If you say to a man, "I need you," and his eyes look pan-
icked, then definitely he's not the man you belong with.
But if you say to a man, "I need you," and his eyes look
amused, because he knows that you know you don't *really*
need him, but still he's totally turned on that you would say
it because he knows the level on which you *do* mean it, then
I would suggest you take your shoes off and plan to stay
a while.

∞

Dear God,
Please protect and nourish
my beloved.
Surround him with Your power and grace.
Make clear the road that You would have him walk,
easy the goals You accomplish in his life,
and soft the pillow he rests on.
Use me to provide for him
an ever more wonderful life.
Amen

∞

I can see how it's been very hard for men for the last thirty years or so. "No, I don't need you to open the car door for me." (Read: "You jerk.") "No, you are not invited to fix me, you will not be allowed to dominate me, and you better not *dare* put your feet on either my emotional or my material furniture." (Read: "In fact, I'll cut off your you-know-whats if you try.") "No, I do not appreciate your efforts to make things better, because I'm sure it's just another of your patriarchal, domineering, chauvinistic plans masquerading as a solution." (Read: "You realize, of course, that I hate your entire sex.")

And many of these poor guys *got* it. They themselves could see the destructiveness of the brutish, shadow side of the male personality, as much as we could—and they wanted to not be that, as much as we wanted to not be around it. Even this shows a desire to please us, at least subconsciously. Ironically, what then developed in them was the same syndrome with which women have been cursed for centuries: "I'll hide who I really am, so you'll like me." And of course, it didn't work. After we ripped their balls off, we started yelling at them contemptuously, "Why aren't you a man!?!?"

Many men drew inward, shrinking from their own masculinity out of fear *that it might harm someone.* In the name of gentleness, but often stemming more from fear than from genuine tenderness, they shrank from their own male greatness. There are few dangers greater than the danger of an unrecognized belief, and the unrecognized belief that masculinity is somehow corrupt, in and of itself, has crippled both men and women for decades.

Some of the best men among us, the souls most equipped to usher in the romance and spirituality of the era now dawning, often acquiesced to the prejudice against powerful males. They withdrew from what they saw as the rat race, as appalled as we were at the violence and greed of white male power in America. As usual, the judgment was a slash to the heart of both judger and judged. Slowly, silently, and often unconsciously, these men began to mourn the loss of their own vigor and male assertiveness, painfully conflicted about their valid desire and aptitude for material manifestation. They could not obliterate their desire to go, to do, to build empires, to exert power in the world, yet held that desire deep within them like a guilty secret. Having been made to feel wrong, in essence, for the worldly expression of their own masculinity, they attitudinally crouched in a corner, secretly jealous of lesser men.

Often, they don't want to admit it, but they wish that they

had made more money. They don't want to admit it, but they wish now that they *did* have a worldly empire. They don't want to admit it, but they feel embarrassed that they don't have the means to do certain things in the material world. All this can be corrected, of course, as soon as they recognize where they judged a certain trait, thus suppressing their own power to personify it. Forgiveness is the key to healing absolutely everything. What we judge in others, we deny ourselves. What we are willing to bless in others, we will allow ourselves. Judging a trait, even suppressing it, does not transform it. Allowing an energy to emerge, and asking that it be blessed by God and used for His/Her purposes, is the only way to lift it higher.

Not all men who make a lot of money do evil, brutish, domineering things with it—not by a long shot. Not all men who build worldly empires then use their empires to suppress and exploit and manipulate others—not by a long shot. And not all men of worldly means are spiritual morons—not by a long shot.

It's worth mentioning, as well, that not all people who are struggling to survive are so holy and pure. The myth that money is the root of all evil was invented by the master, not the slave, and for the purposes of further enslavement. It is a thought that is sure to quiet the disempowered masses, but at a time like this, when empowerment is the buzz, that thought is being dropped from our minds like chains being thrown off long-bound shoulders. The attachment to money is a danger, as the attachment to anything is a danger. But money, like anything else, can be used in the service of furthering the good. And a lot of what would help the world most, right now, would be well served by an influx of cash.

Money is just a symbol, of course, for a certain kind of worldly power. But particularly for men, it is an important symbol, for it represents the power to wield a certain kind of authority in our society. To pretend otherwise is immature. This is not a negative authority, by the way, but a neutral authority. All of us should feel *authorized* to create. We don't want a world where everyone feels equally disempowered; we want a world where everyone can feel equally empowered to manifest the power of good.

Making men wrong for the worldly expression of their masculine self, in any form, is like making men wrong for an erection. Fine if you want to do that, but don't expect any more babies, or new life, if you do.

The story of Isis and Osiris reveals that the feminine does not just give birth to new life: it restores life where it is broken. Love is a feminine force, not just in women but in men as well, creating not out of "doing" but out of "being"—being loved, being appreciated, being honored, being wanted, being cherished, being respected, and being received at the deepest levels of our souls. That is why the deeper the state of our own emotional and spiritual being, the more of a psychic womb we are for the conception and gestation of an enchanted love.

For the last few decades, many men have supported our journey of mystical feminism, helping give birth to our more liberated identities as their mothers had given birth to them. Upon physical birth, we lie in our mother's arms. Upon spiritual rebirth, the divine mother reaches through the lover to hold us once again.

And now, a new twist in the storyline of our cosmic rebirth is developing, as the souls of so many men among us are silently saying, "I helped birth you. Now please, birth me. Tell me it's okay to be a man, the way I once told you it's okay to be a woman. If you want to know what my dream is, my dream is to be me. Hold a space for who I am, and I will hold a space for who you are. Otherwise, I will never know myself. And until I know myself, I cannot know you."

To know each other is the only reason we're here. To truly

know each other is to love each other, and to love each other is to know and love God. To know and love God is to co-create with Him, a world on earth as it is in heaven. Hallelujah, we will be naked and unembarrassed. Hallelujah, we will play in the garden. Hallelujah, we will all be free.

෨

So rest in me, and I will rest in you. The rest is in the hands of God. . . .

෨

Dear God,
Please remove from me
my resistances to love.
Make straight my path
to the heart of my beloved.
Reveal to me the meaning
of this ride that we are on.
Amen

5

⁓

Love and Fire

You know what I see in you? Not only the weakened, but also the strong. Not only the wounded, but also the healed. Not only the old, but also the new. Enter with me into a dazzling present, to be with me, now, who we have never allowed ourselves to be before.

New water pours over us, as we surrender to the wave. We will wash ourselves clean of the yesterdays that stick to us. This is not death. We are not drowning.

Forget with me, my darling. Forget with me what never was.

⁓

A FRIEND OF MINE e-mailed me to say he was in love. This was it. This was the real one, the maddeningly rapturous, complete and total experience of love he'd been waiting for his entire life.

Several months later, I was speaking to him and asked him how his love affair was doing.

"I'm still in there," he said. "But it's hard. It's bringing up all my issues."

"Like what?" I asked.

"Like tolerance. Anger. Enmeshment. Judgment. My mother."

"Wow," I said. "That certainly sounds like a lot of fun."

"I have gotten totally in touch with how I responded to my mother's attempted suicide when I was four years old," he said. "I decided back then that I would take care of her, no matter what, so she wouldn't leave me. And now, when someone abandons me or doesn't act the way I think they should, I just die. I used to attack people when they did that, because I would go into denial over it and pretend it wasn't happening, but now I know I need to get in touch with my feelings no matter what, but even when I get in touch with the feelings, then I have to not attack or judge because otherwise I'll just turn the other person off and then they'll leave me all over again and that's my mother."

"How fun!" I said. "And your girlfriend? What is she like?"

"She's intense. She's powerful. She's angry. She's selfish. She's narcissistic. But she's really doing the work. I have never seen anybody do the work the way she's doing. She's looking deep into issues that I'm only just beginning to question. It's amazing. All of her incest and abandonment issues are right in her face. She's in therapy and looking at these things, and I understand it makes her totally self-absorbed to be dealing so deep with those issues right now, but I get jealous because I want more of her attention and then that brings up all my abandonment issues. We fight on an average of once a week. She doesn't take any of my shit. But it's tiring after a while. I really don't know how long this ride is gonna last."

"So! . . ." I exclaimed, exhausted from merely hearing the story. "Have you seen any good movies lately?"

Hearing my friend tell the story of his love affair, I had my own thoughts about what issues were being brought to the fore. To me, they were in some ways different from his. I don't minimize the need for psychological work, but as necessary as it can be, purely analytical understanding is not the ultimate meaning of intimacy. In fact, I think we should avoid the temptation to pathologize relationships so much. It can tempt us to insidiously avoid the real experience of love.

At the heart of love lies an irreducible mystery. To demystify love is to lose it. Its mystery provides its vital power to enchant us, to touch us, and to heal us. In far too many relationships, the mystery is squeezed out of love. Plans, form, analysis, definition—they can all be used to block love's spiritual outpour. Mystery is fragile and demands our protection. We must surrender ourselves to a higher drama if we would drink of the divine.

Beyond the mortal mind is the realm of immortal spirit, with a different story to tell from the hysterical drama that we call life. I heard a different story from the one my friend was relaying, as he told me of his relationship. It was the story of a generation with a desperate need to apply spiritual principles to our romantic pursuits. Truths such as forgiveness; learning to live in the moment; knowing that we right the wrongs of the past through right, compassionate living in the present; respecting the mystery that brings us together; listening to the wisdom of the heart; not hiding behind psychological analysis; seeking God's grace; creating emotional safety for ourselves and for each other; avoiding the temptation to judge and find fault; cradling the broken other in our arms; and pouring on support and approval, in an effort to bless and heal us both.

❧

I warn you: this will not be easy. I warn you: this will take some work. I warn you: love will burn you up. Are you ready to be burned, or would you rather just grow old?

❧

Jean-Paul Sartre once wrote, "Hell is other people."
And so is heaven.
Relationships *can* be hell. Someone isn't getting enough time or attention, someone else isn't getting enough freedom or space. Someone's controlling; someone else is withholding. Someone's crying and trying to get in; someone else is sighing and trying to get out. Over and over, we are emotionally bombarded. Often we wonder, "Why do I bother?"

Yet every once in a while, there is a burst of starlight: a minute, an hour, perhaps a day or year or even much longer, when love is perfect. We are truly seen by someone and that someone loves what he or she sees. The very air becomes a moving sidewalk as we stride from one right moment to another, completing each other's sentences, holding each other's dreams. Our very molecules seem to know each other. In that one moment, or on that one day, we finally feel not alone on this earth after all.

But then reality sets in, or actually, *nonreality* sets in. Love is the ultimate, God-created, unchangeable reality in the universe, but the world we have made for ourselves does not acknowledge or reflect that. With our free will, we have established an alien mental kingdom ruled not by love but by thoughts of fear. Love does not feel at home in the world of fear, and that is because it is not. Lasting love can be very hard to achieve on this plane, running as it does so counter to the grain of the emotional status quo. The ways of love can feel almost unnatural. We have manufactured for ourselves, in this illusionary world, a kind of ersatz love. It is based more on tolerance than on real acceptance, more on form than on content, and more on the joining of bodies than on the joining of spirits. And as long we keep things shallow, as long as there is no run for the mountaintop experience of love, then these relationships have a fairly good chance of surviving.

But if you dare to say, "No, I want more," then you are confronting the ego and demanding the joy that is your natural birthright as a child of God. If you have the courage to stand up and consciously declare that the limits to love in this world do not work for you, that you choose to experience the lifting of the veil while you are still alive, then you have taken on the forces of fear.

And fear will answer you. "Fine," it will say. "Love deeply, if you want to. See if I care. But watch that wall of fire in front of you, and on your left and on your right. It will consume you, of course. But by all means, go ahead and try to walk right through."

That fire does consume, but grace bestows upon us a titanium personality structure invincible enough to withstand the heat. Two souls genuinely combining spiritual forces generate—quite literally—the power of God. That power is reflected in the material world. Both nuclear fusion and nuclear fission are physical reflections of the extraordinary potential for both destructiveness and creativity, when two units of life either separate or merge. Relationships can be powerfully bad, and they can be powerfully good, but they cannot be powerless.

Love can be a huge mountain, a gentle garden, a raging storm, a cool breeze, or a perfect bath. But there is always fire somewhere nearby. There is always the red-hot stuff of the soul's initiation. If there isn't fire, then it isn't love. It might be a marriage that lasts forever. It might have all the signs of what the world calls a "successful relationship." But if it doesn't insist that you move to your next level, if it doesn't take your heart and make it explode in a million pieces, only to fall back together again in some moment of enlightened understanding, then you haven't really loved. You've done the bourgeois thing perhaps, but let's not call that love.

Any time there is a chance for deep love, there is standing in front of that love a wall of fire. That fire might take the form of something burning within you—an inner condition—or it might take the form of an outer circumstance. But there is never love without fire. To the mystic, the presence of that fire does not say, "Go away." To the mystic, the presence of that fire says, "Here, if you are strong enough to take it, is love."

Chaka Khan sang a song years ago, in which she proclaimed that she was willing to "go through the fire" for her man. The truth is, it is that fire that molds us. The fire is not the danger of the relationship, but its greatest gift. It does not burn up the essential self, but rather it burns up everything else. When a wall of fire stands in front of you, but one you truly love is on the other side of it, then reaching through the fire for your beloved's hand will make you a magical being who can walk through fire without getting burned. At that point, we take on another frequency of consciousness. When we can do that, we can do most anything.

The world gives prizes for many things. There's a prize for the best everything that anyone can imagine. But the only prize for the artist at love is the thrill of knowing you've made it through that fire to the other side. There is no worldly prize that can match the thrill of this accomplishment, and the smile it brings to two people's faces.

The thrill of knowing that that fire is behind you, that the metal in your heart is now turned to gold, makes of a relationship a sacred chalice. Humanity's romantic energies are ready for that chalice; we have the water, we just haven't had the cup. A civilization that doesn't acknowledge the sacred in any meaningful, practical way, but rather leaves it in a completely dry and sexless context, has no guidebook for sacred romance. It doesn't see the divine in most anything truly human, so how could it see the divine in the most human thing in the world?

We will bathe in magic water and we will allow the sun to dry our skin. We will close our eyes and take in new light. We will listen to the whispering counsel of angels.

We will look at each other with the eyes of the new. We will honor each other with the crown of the sky. We will touch each other with the touch of the earth. And love will be our medicine. God will smile, and we will smile, and the world itself will become more glad.

Come with me. I want to show you love.

✧

The biggest block to love is the human personality. I drove up to my daughter's school one day, and I saw a little girl, around age five, talking to a little boy. Talking isn't the right word, really. It was a perfect flow of energy between these two little people. She was open, smiling, flirting before she could even know what the word means. And he was a little cocky, just eating it up. Another twenty years, and—barring some dramatic shift—the world will surely have done its thing to these two children. The same conversation will be laden with emotional issues.

I stared longingly for a moment. That little girl was so unguarded and yet so safe. She had nothing to fear here because fear had not occurred to her yet, or to him. She was completely vulnerable, completely undefended, completely adoring, and completely herself. I felt jealous. Each of us carries a little girl or little boy like that inside ourselves, like a remembrance of our lost innocence. We want to be that free, but who has the guts anymore? We want to be that adoring, but who has the skill? We want to be that innocent, but we can't remember how.

I was reminded of a painting I saw once at a museum in New York City. A young man and woman are running naked through the woods in some mythical setting. They both have perfect, sensual bodies, yet there is no sense of sexual prowess or shame. They have the smiles of angels. I stood for a long time before that painting, wondering, "Does that really exist? Did it ever? Is it just an ideal? Can we love as adults, yet reclaim the trust of a child? Can we be this, and also that? Can we live in this world, and in Eden simultaneously?"

Perhaps we can, if we try. If we let fall into the sea what is ready to fall, then ground that is new will arise to the surface. Paradise exists. It is merely submerged.

ↄ

Dear God,

I used to pray to You because I was lonely,

but then You came to me and I was lonely no more.

Then I prayed to you to make me better,

and you came to me and healed my heart.

Now I ask you, dear God,

for a glorious mission.

May I contribute to the life of another,

in the deepest way,

the most holy way,

the most loving way,

that together we might serve You more.

May I help a beloved

grow closer to You,

may a beloved help me

grow closer to You.

May I delight in my partner,

and my partner delight in me,

that Your light which unites us

might light up the world.

Thank you, God.

Amen

❧

Now that you have said that prayer, you might wish to prepare your inner room. Write down on a piece of paper the characteristics of your personality that you most want transformed by the Holy Spirit. Own these things, take responsibility for your defects, and then surrender them to God. Ultimately, all work is inner work.

Now you might wish to look around your house. Is it a place where your love would find comfort? Are the items here for his or her delight? Is there an area of your existence that would keep love away? Deal with these things now, for his or her footsteps are near.

Be patient and be calm. For the hour is nigh for all of us.

❧

And I am all fitted now, in a gown of light. My sisters and I have dancing shoes, and we dance most every night. Musicians play, and we sing our songs, and breathe life into the words. Our little sisters come and join us as we prepare the otherworld.

Know you that we wait for you? We do. We do.
And are you prepared to dance?

ॐ

AND THEN, the beloved. She comes. People had said you might meet her in this way or that, but when the day arrived, she just appeared. Funny. She's not who you would have thought capable of snatching your heart from your chest.

Love is simpler than it appears, in this complicated world of ours. The secret of love is to tell the beloved how wonderful he or she is, constantly and sincerely, at least a million times every day. Give and then give some more and then give a little more than that. To the extent that love has dried up in my life, it was always because I became miserly with my expression of compassion. To the extent that love has blossomed in my life, it was always because I expanded my willingness to express the love that often cowers like a child in a corner of my heart. I have learned that everyone has that corner, and the childlike place where we cower within it. When we honestly speak from that place in ourselves, we encounter that place in someone else, and then two frightened children become two courageous adults, with a very adult capacity to love and to be loved.

Dear God,

I don't wish to be a child anymore.

I don't wish to be held back anymore.

I don't wish to waste my life.

Deliver me to new realms,

repair me where I am broken,

and ready my heart for everything.

Thank you, God.

Amen

6

∾

Grown-ups in Love

And when I reached for you, you said no, you can do better. I said I cannot, I cannot, I am tired and I cannot try anymore.

After all this time, you told me, you can come to me the way I want to come to you.

And so I did. And I will do it again, and again and again, for as long as we both shall live. . . .

∾

AUTHOR AND PSYCHOTHERAPIST Pat Allen has written that a man's greatest psychic need is to have his thoughts respected, and that a woman's greatest psychic need is to have her feelings cherished. I have heard many opinions expressed about that thought, but for me it has been a ray of light. Knowing it has transformed my relationships.

I grew up in a cultural environment where everyone had an Aunt Bessie, or her equivalent. She had a heart of gold, but boy, was she tough. She would say and do things that people who didn't know her—or didn't come from our culture— might not have known what to do with, but people in the family would just laugh affectionately and say, "That Bessie! What a character!" She was the strongest as well as the most loving member of the family. In fact, she held the whole thing together.

She grew up in poverty, but her sons grew up to be men who brought home half a million dollars each year. This left her unfazed. "So I should show respect? Don't talk to me from respect! Oh my God, why didn't you eat?!? You don't like my cooking? Max, you look sick. Are you sick?! Is there something you're not telling me?"

I didn't realize it when I was growing up, but Aunt Bessie was basically my role model for a powerful woman. That's how the women who ran things around me behaved! What did I know from anything else? Respect for a man's thoughts and achievements? What, are you kidding? Do you know how hard I worked today? And Bessie wasn't exactly emotionally vulnerable. Her family had fled *pogroms*, for God's sake. Softness wasn't one of her tissues.

So I, like so many women of my generation, between the trials of our grandmothers and trials of our own, grew up with scales on our skin and claws growing out of our fingers. Every woman I know has a version of the Aunt Bessie story. And we didn't know we were damaged; we thought we were strong.

According to Pat Allen, our parents' generation didn't exactly have things figured out right, either. Fathers patted their daughters on the back at puberty, saying, "There you go! You can do things as well as a boy can!" leading us to believe that *achieving* something would earn us love from the men in our lives. And boy, were we wrong.

Mothers of that generation, on the other hand, made the opposite mistake, coddling their adolescent sons' feelings at exactly the time when those young men should have been heading for the proverbial woods, passing ritualistically from boyhood to manhood, learning to trust their own choices. What a mess we became, with women wearing all the emotional armor and men dropping all their emotional baggage at the feet of women who are *not* their mothers. "My Daddy said he'd love me if I made an A+—why don't you?" meets, "My mother indulged me when I acted like a child—why don't you?"

Because the beloved is not your father; he is the man who has arrived at your side.

Because the beloved is not your mother; she is the woman who has arrived at your side.

The first thing real love will do is make you grow up. And then it will show you how to enjoy the experience.

❧

OFTEN TWO ADULTS come together and simply reenact their childhood dramas ad infinitum. One rather common passion play takes place when a man who never really grew up falls in love with a woman who thinks that maybe she can *make* him grow up.

A woman who tries to do a man's emotional work *for* him has chosen to play the role of his mother. It can be very tempting for a woman to do a man's psychic work in a relationship, until she recognizes that (1) she *can't;* and (2), even if she could, if she were an adult herself, she wouldn't want to. Mothering a man by definition cancels out his manhood and fortifies his dysfunction. A grown man's inability to take responsibility for his own thoughts, feelings, and actions is neurotic to begin with, and a woman trying to compensate for his lack by putting more of herself forward is matching his neurosis with her own.

If his mother didn't release him when she should have, the answer is not for you to carry him. The answer is for someone to release him now. Until a man makes an essential break with his boyhood, he will not have the muscles for real manhood, or for real love. He will not know how to reach far enough for love, and women around him will always be tempted to respond by reaching too far. This spells emotional disaster for both.

A woman cannot win by mothering a man because a man does not want to sleep with his mother. A woman who emotionally does too much *for* a man will always end up losing him.

"But if I don't do it *for* him—if I don't call him when he stops calling, if I don't make him discuss his feelings and show him what he's doing, if I don't explain to him what he's doing wrong in the relationship when he obviously doesn't

have a clue—then the relationship will end! It won't continue!" some women then say.

And that, perhaps sadly, is precisely the point. If a man you
want isn't coming toward you, it might be time to grieve, but
it isn't time to reach for his lapels. He's not coming toward you
for one reason, and that is this: *he doesn't want to.* If you seduce,
manipulate, strategize, or otherwise try to make something
happen that he would not have initiated on his own, then one
of two things will happen: One, you'll fail, which will ultimately make you feel humiliated, rejected, and embarrassed.
This will also make you increasingly wary of being bold in situations where it *is* appropriate to be bold, meaning there will
be a mess to clean up from this relationship in ones not even
here yet. Or, two, you'll succeed, but it is bound to be a pyrrhic
victory. Someday he will figure out what you've done, and it
will destroy a fundamental trust between you. If he consciously figures it out, then he will be angry and he will leave.
If he merely registers what occurred on an unconscious level,
then he will still be angry, and emotionally, he will still leave.

For in that situation, he will not have come to you freely, as
a man, but will simply have acquiesced to your willfulness.
He will not have genuinely surrendered his heart. You did not
win his love, then; you merely temporarily outsmarted him.

When he realizes this, he will put his heart back in his pocket, and it is unlikely that it will ever be entrusted to your hands again.

Why would a woman try to manipulate a man into loving her? At bottom, because she is desperate. She wants a grand, passionate love in her life, which everyone does. Such a possibility is impressed upon our souls, and each of us has wandered the earth looking for such love since the day we were born. There's nothing wrong with the desire itself. What is wrong is trying to cut corners to get it. Love is granted freely by the universe, but right relationship is earned. Love itself is free-floating energy, but relationship is a worldly container for it. That container must be built of integrity, righteousness, and compassion or the energy becomes destructive. Violation of self or others is registered by the universe, duly recorded, and sent right back to us with karmic precision.

The psychological imperative for a man, when he is interested in a woman, is the opposite of a woman's when she is interested in a man. Unless she's told you not to, it's a good idea to help her notice the way you hung the moon and the graceful way you put the stars in the sky. Most women carry a chorus from *My Fair Lady* around in our heads: "If you're in love, show me."

A woman in love, however, needs to avoid the temptation to act like a man. It doesn't work to try to *convince* a man that you are the woman of his dreams. Flirt, yes; connive, no. When a woman connives, she has not yet learned that if a train doesn't stop at our station, it's simply because it's not our train. She wants to flag down the conductor and convince him to stop here, even if his own map says that he should just keep going. Sadly, she doesn't realize that there's another train trying to come toward her, unable to get into her station because a train that doesn't even belong there is being delayed there by her intensity.

Sometimes a man isn't coming toward you not because he doesn't love you, but because he does not know how. Or he is too afraid. That can be very true and very sad; but if you are to be his woman, you cannot be his tutor. The bottom line in love is not whether someone loves you, but whether someone *chooses* you. The second biggest mistake—after acting like a man's mother—is acting like his teacher. Put bluntly, he doesn't get it up for her, either. When a sacred, honoring, and respectful context for love has been established, then indeed we can take on the various roles that make up the many facets of love. Parent and teacher and lover and friend can all be part of love's emotional mosaic. But if all those roles show up too early, they can grow fuzzy and muddy and diminish love's strength. The dominant psychic grooves between two people are set at the beginning of a relationship, and the tracks of both parent and teacher, while perhaps attracting someone in the early phases of a relationship, are bound to repel that person later on.

Whom we teach, or mother, or help too much, we have a semblance of control over. That's one of the reasons those roles are such tempting parts to play for those of us who are ourselves afraid of real intimacy. But if you give in to that temptation, the joke will one day be on you, as surely as Eliza broke free of Professor Higgins. It is in the natural order of things for everyone to finally grow up and achieve his or her own strength.

Men and women's souls are in relationships to *grow*, not to avoid growth. Something in each of us knows this and wants that growth more than anything else. That is why, ultimately, we are most attracted to people who will *not* indulge our games.

The masculine initiates and the feminine receives. Both men and women carry masculine and feminine energy, but in a relationship, one partner primarily plays one part or another. Unconsciously, feminine and masculine attract, while two feminines—or two masculines—cancel each other out. This is as true in gay as in heterosexual relationships.

If a woman is playing the initiator in a relationship—the male, aggressive role—then a man can only stay in her space at the expense of his masculinity. If he gives in to a woman's psychological demands, he is playing female to her male. Even if he is willing to surrender that in order to satisfy her, a woman isn't usually happy with a man if he arrives at her door like a puppy dog.

If you can lasso a man, then what you get when you do get him is not a man but a boy. The woman who refuses to even try to lasso him is the only one with the real chance of ever getting him. With her, he is at least likely to say, "Hey, why didn't you tug when I let my side of the rope fall? I'm used to women picking up the slack!" That woman's answer would be, "Because I didn't want to. I only play with grown men."

At this point, some women would be thinking, "Yes, but my man doesn't know *how* to be a man!" *Exactly!* Only a woman who has high standards, who has no interest in anything but the most adult interaction between a man and a woman, has the capacity to inspire a man to learn how to act like one. A man will not be attracted, or at least he will not remain attracted, to a woman who emotionally tries to do his work *for* him, because in his heart what he wants most is the experience of his own manhood. He is unconsciously seeking initiation into new levels of masculine strength, and any woman who indulges his childish behavior cannot be his initiatory experience.

What ultimately attracts both men and women is the fire of initiation, the unconscious lure of the situation that represents the next stage of our personal growth. But the only way we can teach others is by conscientiously trying to learn our own lessons in their presence. Finding and living our own truth—not telling others what theirs should be—is the greatest gift we can give to others. Psychologically it's important that we stay on our own side of the net in a relationship, doing our own work and focusing on our own reactions. If the other person doesn't reach over for us, we have to accept that there's not really a game here.

A man who doesn't want you right now is not the man for you right now. Trying to make him into that creates a negative loop in relationships. And what is the way out of that loop? Commit to breaking through it. Recognize your negative thoughts and emotions as addictive patterns, based more on childhood dramas than on the realities of the here and now. Do not underestimate the power of your own self-hatred and its insidious way of leading you into the darkness you so very much want to be free of. Fall to your knees. Ask God to help you.

The experienced doctor can diagnose diseases he or she has seen before, more quickly. When a man comes on strong—but then pulls back at the first sign that he's getting what he asked for—he is announcing that *he is not yet ready for love*. Announce that *you are*, not by co-dependently explaining to him what he obviously doesn't understand, or by trying to get him more hot and interested again. Announce to the *universe* that you are ready for a relationship that is more adult—and not by getting angry at someone who isn't acting like one yet. Anger at a man for doing the boyish thing in love is no more reasonable than anger at a six-year-old for not yet being able to tie a necktie.

Actually, didn't you act childishly yourself, if you rushed in with your heart before it had been proven to you that this was a psychologically and emotionally adult situation? It always helps us to remember that our bodies grow up early, but our hearts and minds and souls can lag far behind. A friend of mine once said, "Women want love as a lifestyle, but men want love as a vacation." I don't think that applies to all men by any means, but it's an interesting statement nevertheless.

Many times men are blamed for not making a trip that they hadn't signed up for in the first place.

Men don't usually lie, unless we've proved to them that the truth makes us hysterical. It's amazing what happens when you ask a man what he wants from a relationship; usually, he'll tell you. But often, if what he says in one way or the other is, "Not all that much, just some fun," we think, "He doesn't really mean that," or "I can change his mind."

Nyet. He probably meant it.

So what a marvelous opportunity this is for two people to grow up. He starts outgrowing those situations where he wasn't adult enough to take on what he himself invited in, and healing from the chronic habit of showing up for something and then wimping out. She starts taking responsibility for the fact that she had a habit of giving her heart to men who *never really said they wanted it.*

We rarely learn our lessons from people who are judging us or blaming us. For instance, if a man drew close to a woman but then failed to honor the depth of their sharing, then he will not see his own behavior clearly if the woman expresses anger at him. He will probably get his lesson *very* clearly, however, from a woman who doesn't find him wrong, so much as, well, weak. She finds it somewhat annoying perhaps, but ulti-

mately simply amusing, that he's so immature at love. *Ouch.*
That's a woman with something to teach a man, not because
she is trying to, but simply because she has learned something
herself. Every man is unconsciously looking for his next rite
of passage. A woman who indulges, or even punishes, his
childish behavior cannot give him that.

Some lessons we learn only when we have done something,
and then upon understanding what we did, start to squirm. A
whole new level of humility, and then adulthood, starts to
happen after that.

⁊

MEN LIKE TO HUNT. My mother used to tell me
that, but I thought she didn't understand very much. Now I
am in my forties, and like many other women I know, I finally
understand that in many ways my mother was right. Men
hunt because it is part of the hormonal imprint of the universe that they do so. This isn't control or domination. Actually, it's just *courting.*

A man doesn't ultimately desire what he didn't have to
work for, at least a little. Women often complain, "He
worked to get me, but once he got me completely, he stopped

being interested." So whose fault was that!? God help us, our mothers were right—we give too much too easily. A man should *never* have to totally stop working to figure out his woman, not if the woman wants him to remain interested. That doesn't mean he can never relax, but simply that a fascinating woman is high maintenance and doesn't apologize for the fact. Does a Mercedes apologize for being high maintenance? Does a Jaguar? Does an expensive house? Please. To a male who is an adult at love, there's no relaxing *until* he knows that he can get away with very little immature behavior with this woman. He can relax into the sure and certain knowledge that she will forever be fueling the part of him that doesn't *want* to stop working, that doesn't *want* to stop hunting, because *he doesn't ever want to stop being fascinated.*

And why should he? A woman who knows who she is *is* endlessly fascinating. And a *man* who knows who he is knows this about women.

A woman should always be just a step ahead of a man; he should never know everything she's thinking, and if she's truly current with herself he won't. This isn't game playing, by the way; it's dancing. It's enchantment. A man can feel it when a woman desires him yet doesn't need him. It drives him crazy, but in a way that he loves.

If God comes first in our lives, then we are clear from whence we derive our sustenance. God is the only partner we *need*. The human at our side is a partner we *desire*. A clear difference between the two puts our inner world in balance, and then, and only then, can love rule all things.

God gives to us, constantly and unendingly. When open to receive His gifts, we initiate the next phase of His giving. The eternal dance of giving and receiving is built into the spiritual rhythm of things.

Receiving is as blessed as giving, and at bottom they are the same thing. When we can't receive, we are like people who, though fed, have malfunctioning digestive systems and therefore remain unnourished. On an emotional level, the reason this is so important is that emotionally hungry people are angry. We are angry about feeling unfed, but meanwhile, people right in front of us might have been feeding us constantly, as best they can, and are starting to wonder why we ourselves are so ungrateful, bratty, and ungiving.

A man once walked out of my house declaring angrily, "Nothing I ever did was good enough for you, Marianne." I remember weakly crying out to him from the doorway, "Everything you ever did was good enough." He responded,

"Too bad you never told me that, babe." After that, not surprisingly, he was gone and gone for good.

I was like someone at my own birthday party who, instead of receiving gifts from guests and enjoying the surprise and affection poured into each one, had a list of what gifts I wanted and what they should look like, and I kept tabs on whether or not they were good enough. Sometimes people gave me magnificent gifts, but I was too wrapped up in myself to even see that there was a gift here at all. Someone might have given me one thing, but because I thought I was looking for something else, I missed the gift entirely. Most of us have been on one side of this equation or the other at some point in our lives. A man once said to me regarding our past experience together, "I had two tickets to the World Series and I didn't even know we were playing baseball."

Yet if all people truly are is love—and all we ever really do is extend that love—then everyone is gifting us on some level or another, at every moment of our lives. Mystical power lies in asking ourselves what the gift is, and then opening ourselves to receive it.

Clearly some people are more generous than others, and sometimes the gift is in what we learn from an experience, not in how good it feels. Sometimes a gift can come in a very odd package, indeed! But still, if we train our minds to ask, in any situation, "What is the gift here? Am I acknowledging the gift? Am I receiving the gift?," then the tenor of our emotional nature begins to shift. We're not just standing in front of the drinking fountain of life; we are choosing to drink the living water.

Someone who does not know how to receive love will, of course, end up feeling unloved. We then grow bitter or cynical, making us less and less attractive, keeping love at a distance, and bolstering our belief that a loving universe isn't really that loving in *our* case. Uh, right. . . .

The truth is that love is always pouring forth upon us, but our belief that the purpose of relationships is to serve our needs as we define them often blocks reception. Asking only, "What am I getting here?" is death to love because it puts all responsibility on the other person. Asking, "What lesson is there for me to receive here?," however, is a mystical key that unlocks your own heart. And *that* is our greatest need—to experience the things that make us more loving and more lovable.

What we experience and what we receive are in many ways our own choices. The same experience will be experienced completely differently, depending on the mind of the one who experiences it. One woman might say about a man who left her, "He abandoned me." She will then have even more data to support her "abandonment issue." Another woman, however, or the same woman once she has grown bored enough with that idea, might say, "He was being himself, going through his stuff, and this time I didn't choose to see that as abandonment. I blessed his path, respected his choice, and was grateful for what I had received from him." When heart chatter replaces mind chatter, the power of love flows with full force.

To the extent that our mental focus is on blessing rather than condemnation, we are in our natural state. Every thought and every word determines that. And we are responsible for the conversations we engage in; they are heard by the universe itself. People who say to us, "He abandoned you. You should feel angry," are our allies, perhaps, but not necessarily our spiritual companions. The *I Ching* points out that even thieves have allies. It is possible, in fact, to validate someone's feelings while at the same time validating their capacity to move beyond those feelings. People who say to us, "I know you're in pain, but could we look at this another way? Could we find a way to bless him?" are our true spiritual companions, because they are helping us find the spirit of love within ourselves.

In the *state* of love, we are magnets for love. We are literally more lovable and more enjoyable to love. Love with us becomes intoxicating, and that is how it should be.

❦

ONE OF THE enchanted keys to love is learning how to *receive* a lover. You inwardly bow to the spirit of one who has graced your path. It's much like receiving a guest at the front door, making the person feel more welcome in your home. While none of this occurs on the outer levels, it is felt within, and binds your lover's heart to you.

We cannot truly receive someone until we have learned, with grace and gratitude, to receive his or her many gifts to us. The lover's smile is a gift. The lover's thoughts are a gift. The lover's work is a gift. The lover's advice (yes, I did say that) is a gift. And if you don't think that, then why are you with this person? And if your answer to that question is that you really don't know, then perhaps if you start to think this way, their gifts will become more attractive to you.

I once heard Pat Allen say that men produce into women's appetites. Men are by nature producers, and one of the things they produce into is female desire. From our sexual lives to our emotional lives, that is an archetypal pattern of great beauty and significance. But a woman who blocks the gift, by either minimizing it, demanding it, or in some other way resisting it, makes it difficult for a man to experience this essential aspect of himself. That then denies both of them the thrill of this particular part of their dance together.

We are in relationships to experience aspects of ourselves that cannot be experienced when we are alone. Some of those aspects are facets of our more solitary existence, expanded to include another being.

I used to feel that prayer and meditation were basic to my life when I was not in relationship, but didn't fully appreciate their power to guide me when I was. That changed as I began to realize how much of relationship work is inner work. We sometimes seek to keep from God the areas that we think aren't spiritual enough for His attention! Or perhaps, we try to hide them from Him because we're scared of what He might say. After all, who among us was raised to think God would care about our date last night, much less that He wouldn't judge us for what we might have done on it! Once I finally got over all that, I began to find myself in almost constant conversation with God about things that mattered very deeply to me, indeed.

"So then, God, when he said that, I got totally reactive. I knew I shouldn't have, and I knew that I was judging him, but it's like a part of myself I couldn't control. Please God, heal me of the part of myself that keeps doing this all the time."

Things like that. And then the same situation would present itself, and the next day's conversation would go something like, "You know, Lord, when he said that again, it wasn't too bad. I mean, I wasn't Ms. Serene exactly, but I wasn't hysterical either. Please help me get better at this."

Finally, the same situation would happen again and I would feel like I had received a true healing. And I knew where it had come from. More and more, I began to see my meditation and prayer times as opportunities to commune with God regarding all, not just some, of the issues I was dealing with in my life.

Spiritual practice rests on inner stillness, and stillness is the root of personal power. From within that space, we visit the inner temple of God. It is an underground sanctum that exists in all of us because He placed it there. When we pray and meditate, the mind is naturally drawn to its Source. There we find strength and serenity and guidance and love. Just spending time in that place draws love to us, as everyone is subconsciously seeking that peace within themselves, and we gravitate toward those who have already achieved it. When we think about the beloved while in sacred space, asking that our perceptions of each other be lifted up to God, it is as though a blessing has been cast over the relationship. Stillness draws love to us, and draws our hearts together. Whom we have found in God's stillness we have truly found.

Ultimately, I learned that I need the sanctuary of God's love not just in my own life; a couple needs it as well. Just as old-fashioned homes often used to contain chapels, every romantic relationship should have a chapel space, a place where we turn to each other and say, "Let's pray." Here we pray together in the morning. Here we go together, to surrender our anger and resentments. Here we go with our perceptions of each other and our decisions we need to make as a couple. Here we go at the end of the day. Here we surrender the relationship itself, and ask that it be used for God's purposes. An enchanted love cannot exist without regular visits to the heart of enchantment.

The enchanted lover is able to just *stand in the light* of someone else's love. For women, this is particularly significant. Men are willing to fall all over themselves to give to a woman, but some women don't know how to allow that to happen, simply because they do not know how to be still. We might feel embarrassed or inadequate when a man is coming toward us, and then defend against the moment. We start chattering away, or saying, "No, no, no," when instead we should just be smiling and serenely basking in the glow of a man's input. If he keeps giving, and we keep not receiving, then ultimately he will lose all interest in trying because his joy is in giving, and giving to a brick wall is a drag.

I remember vividly a situation I experienced once in my early twenties. I witnessed two people, ten or twenty years older than myself, encounter each other in the kitchen of someone's house. They were newly in love, and I was struck by her response to him when he looked at her as though to say, "I don't know what to say, but I'm absolutely crazy about you." Her response was total stillness, a mysterious aspect that looked to me as though she were saying, "I don't know what to say either, but there's no way in hell I'm gonna pretend I do, and mess up this moment by saying something stupid." I can only assume they stood in some miraculous bubble that surrounded only the two of them, but in that moment, the intensity and purity of their connection healed everyone in the room.

I write books and give lectures, so obviously I appreciate

the power of words. But what I appreciate equally, particularly as a woman, is the power of silence. Personally, I don't know if any man has gone too far out of his way to hear me speak, but I know of more than one who crossed an ocean to be with me when I'm quiet. There's nothing more powerful than a woman who knows how to contain her power and not let it leak, standing firmly within it in mystery and silence. A woman who talks too much sheds her allure. If a woman wants a man to produce, she should contribute to the dynamic by which he feels naturally compelled to do so. Be still, and know. Know you are beautiful. Know he is good. Know you are gifted. Know he is smart. Know you are a blessing to him, as he is a blessing to you. Know that God is with you both. Knowledge in stillness is itself a mystical power. It attracts harmony and brings perfection to all things. There is more fullness in the apparent emptiness of the cosmic void than in all the material world.

A quarterback has to receive the ball before he can run with it. The reception itself must be alert and dynamic, and there is a relationship equivalent to this. If you are a woman, you might take a solid, still moment to breathe in the sweetness of a compliment that a man just gave you. *He will feel you doing that. It feeds him to know that he just fed you.* You are then more likely to say something in response to the compliment that completely knocks his socks off. You might say sweetly, "Well, I might be good, but believe me, you're better," and because you came from a dynamic stillness when you said this, the chances are better that there's a look on your face that makes him want to do whatever he has to do to continue this ride through the hall and into the bedroom, out into the garden, and up into the sky. And all the time that this is happening, you almost can't believe how easy it is, just taking in the light of the sun and allowing it to warm you. You light up like the sun yourself. Then watch how your beloved receives the light, feels your warmth, kisses your fingers, and makes clear how much he cherishes your heart.

That's when you know you're in the flow of love, on the magic carpet, in the multiple you-know-what's, and it begins to dawn on you that the universe is built to support this going on forever. If we can practice these baby steps, even one conversation at a time where we are able to allow the force of love to do its thing, where we give so much and receive so much and love so much and allow so much that our circuits are exploded and completely rewired, then we can imagine the possibility that someday all of life will be this way. Love will then simply describe the way things are, not just the way that we dream of them being. We will dream our dreams in an awakened state. We will all know laughter as we have never known it before, and our hunger and tears and frustration and pain will disappear forever. We will have outgrown them. We will have let them go.

We will have loved our way to the other side.

Dear God,
Please help me see
that only Love is real.
Please help me see
that my brother is innocent.
Please take me to heaven
while on this earth,
and then, dear Lord,
please keep me there.
Amen

7

&

Grace and Forgiveness

&

Turn off the lights or keep them on. Either way, I will see you.

Call me back or do not call back. Either way, I will hear you.

Tell me yes or tell me no. Either way, I will love you.

&

FORGIVENESS BLESSES EVERYTHING. It surrounds us with grace.

Forgiveness is not what happens when someone has done something wrong, but you in your spiritual su-

periority have the magnanimity to forgive. That is not forgiveness, but judgment—supercilious and, at its core,
self-righteous.

Real forgiveness, from a metaphysical perspective, means we
realize that only love is real. All the love we have ever received
is real, and all the love we ever gave is real. Everything else is a
hallucination of the mortal mind. This doesn't mean it's not
happening in physical terms, but only that beyond the physical, there is another world. Through the eyes of forgiveness, we
can see that world. Through grace, we can actually go there.

Forgiveness would have us overlook each other's errors, not
in a naïve way but in a wise way. I might register something you
did, and duly note it. But that doesn't mean I have to hold it
against you. The faults of the personality are not sins that God
would punish, but rather mistakes that He would correct. And
God would have us love as He loves, in order to achieve His
peace. Forgiveness is a divine corrective that lifts us above the
pain of life and delivers us to higher, sweeter ground.

Forgiveness does not mean we lack boundaries, standards,
or principles. God's love does not destroy our brain cells; it
hardly makes us stupid. Forgiveness doesn't make us weaker
but very much stronger, as it brings our personalities into
alignment with the knowledge of the soul.

The key to forgiveness is not to *seek* the innocence of the beloved but to *assume* the innocence of the beloved. The closer we get to someone, the more temptation there will always be to interpret that person's behavior in a judgmental or defensive way. Making forgiveness a fundamental commitment is key to an enchanted love.

Within each of us there is an innocent place, unchanged by our mistakes. Knowing this is the antidote to the darkness of the world, as it stands for the possibility of transformation and renewal. It repudiates the insidious ways that the ego mind would always have us attack each other, in large ways and small. International and domestic conflicts emerge from the same point, and will end in the same point. Forgiveness is the salvation of the human race.

"He has a lot of issues." "She's holding you emotionally hostage." "This is a very co-dependent relationship." "He clearly takes you for granted." How often have we said those words, or heard them? And how often, in fact, they're very true. But psychological relevance can be a double-edged sword; if we're not careful, it's just another temptation to surrender to the spiritually barbaric urge to attack a brother, yet pretend we didn't. We claim then that guilt is not the issue. But it's always the issue. The thought that someone is guilty is the cornerstone of hell. The thought that someone is innocent is the cornerstone of heaven. And heaven and hell aren't after we die; heaven and hell are right here, right now.

Romance can be a holy place, dedicated to the experience of heaven on earth. But that can only occur if the perception of our mutual innocence is a sacred commitment. Ironically, and devastatingly, how often an intimate relationship is anything but that. How often it becomes the most violent of places, where emotional knives come out of many hidden pockets, and gashes to the heart are common. For those of us who have suffered those wounds, or even inflicted them on others, another alternative presents itself: to make our intimate relationship a sanctuary from guilt. Yes, we will fall short of that. Yes, we will forsake this commitment and have to come back to our hearts. But as soon as two people speak their word, saying, "Our commitment is to the experience of our mutual innocence," there is a grace and protection around the relationship that would not have been there otherwise.

It's so obvious that all of us have suffered, and all of us have made mistakes in life. Yet all of us are trying our best. We can change our perception regarding the nature of human error, knowing that what is not love is but a call for love. Why

not—if instead of mistrusting you—I assume you're
wounded, just like me and everyone else? Why not see the
healing of our wounds as the reason we were drawn to each
other? An intimate relationship will either magnify our guilt
or magnify our innocence, depending on which we are committed to. And in our commitment to each other's innocence
lies our commitment to the love of God. In our forgiveness
lies our healing, and we can only be healed in ourselves of
what we are willing to forgive in others.

I call up in you what I see in you. That does not mean I
will stand for nonsense. It does not mean I will not have
healthy boundaries. It does not mean I will play any games. It
does not mean you can take me for granted, or pull wool over
my eyes, or act like a child. But it means I will keep my loving
eye on you—the real you—and I will always relate to that
person I have seen. *That* you can trust—that I will always be
true to the truth I have seen within you.

Such a love is calling to us. On the other side of the games
we play is the yearning of the soul to play no games at all. As
we heal, we drop them. As we love, we drop them faster. After
decades of dealing with the anger that lay hidden like a can-
cer beneath the surface of our emotional skins, turning all of
us into psychological sumo wrestlers, our healing crisis is be-

ginning to subside. It is no longer winter but the spring of our emotional cycle, and love, quite literally, is in the air.

೧

So open your mouth and take this candy. It is very sweet and it will fill you up. Then, if you do not eat dinner, it will be a very good thing. You do not need dinner. What you need is my sweetness, as I need yours.

We will eat dinner later, when it has become irrelevant.

೧

Soul and personality breathe life into each other. Personality without soul is dry and heavy, but soul without strength of personality can be leaky and lightweight. The integration of the two is a spiritual art form.

My falling madly in love with you is a function of my soul. Yet the fact that I trust myself to surrender to the experience—because I know I won't do anything stupid, that I will not shirk my worldly responsibilities or abdicate my own strength—is because I have confidence in my personality. Often, people avoid psychological work, thinking their soulfulness makes up for any personality "outs." Or conversely, people avoid tending to their own souls because, hey, they're so psychologically hip, who needs divine illumination?

Enchanted intimacy demands mastery in both areas and harmony between them. We are both human and angel, regular guy and mythical king, earth mother and good witch. We are sexual partners having a good time, as well as priests and priestesses opening the doors to sacred realms. Forget one, and you miss the power. Forget the other, and you miss the fun.

If our personalities are honed, but our souls are unprepared, then there might be all kinds of good coming out of a relationship, but there will not be enchantment. On the other hand, if souls are willing, but psyches are unschooled, then the relationship will be splattered with psychic blood soon enough. We enter a tunnel at the beginning of love, functioning as best we can. But we exit the tunnel having been transformed, or we must one day go back and enter again. We are on this earth with work to do, and relationships are like laboratories where the work gets done. Without that work, there is no growth. Being open to work on ourselves, and being open to relationships, amounts ultimately to the same thing. What situation are we ever in that does not involve a relationship in some way?

Some of the most important work we do on romantic relationships is when we're not in them. How we think about love when it is not yet standing in front of us does much to create what it will be when it is. If we've got negative thoughts about intimacy when we're alone, those thoughts are not going to miraculously change when an intimate partner gets here—unless we look at them and let them go. Otherwise, those thoughts will run rampant over a new relationship the way weeds grow rampant over new growth in a garden.

Our fears take many forms in the face of love. Sometimes we feel we're damaged goods of sorts, and who would want us anyway? Thoughts like that can keep love from even entering. People can talk to us till they're blue in the face about how that's just negative thinking, and we've got to change it. Well it *is* negative thinking, but by ourselves we *can't* change it. Let's be very clear about this: Love is a Miracle. It's a God Job. There is a mystery here, and forgetting that places us at a distinct disadvantage in both attracting love and maintaining it.

When love isn't in our lives, it's on the way. If you know that a special guest is coming at five o'clock, do you spend the day messing up the house? Of course not. You prepare. And that is what we should do for love.

⌘

Dear God,
I want to be lovable,
and prepared for a beloved.
Please remove from me the walls
in front of my heart.
Please take from me
the games I play
to deny myself
the joy of life.
Please make me new,
that I might know
an enchanted romance.
Then send to me
my heart's delight.
Please open up the heavenly gates,
that love might flood my soul.
Amen

❧

Partnerships exist, at the highest level, because the celestial staircase stops at a certain point, and we cannot climb farther until we find our beloved. There is just so much work you can do on yourself, sitting alone in your meditation chair. You can say, "Dear God, I hate it when that reactive part of myself comes forward. I can't believe I do this," and God will hear you. But His answer will be that man who says to you, "I do not appreciate your reacting this way, and I will leave you if this behavior continues." Then you learn the lesson on a whole new level, not just abstractly but experientially. You have a chance to actually practice: to play your part in the relationship from a nonreactive place within you, to choose to be your higher self, to build mastery where before you were weak. Your thinking about this mattered; your praying about this mattered; your meditations about this mattered—but stepping up to the plate in the relationship itself will make the ultimate difference between lesson learned and lesson just thought about. Similarly, trying to "fix" that part of yourself through mere psychotherapeutic or self-help approaches probably won't be enough to truly change you, either. It takes real life experience, and the grace of God, to make a person truly change.

❦

PART OF forgiving people is releasing them from our own agendas. This is a million times easier to say than to do.

I was very upset one day because someone hadn't called me when he said he would. A small thing, a drama like that, but it doesn't always feel small when you're in it. My friend hadn't called for a week, though we were mid-sentence in a very intense emotional conversation the last time we had spoken. A huge anxiety began building up inside of me as the week wore on.

I went back and forth between blaming him and blaming myself. The ego doesn't care who you blame, as long as you blame *someone*. But just because a situation is painful, it doesn't mean that someone necessarily has to be at fault. Blame doesn't even have to enter into the calculation. All of us are innocent in God's eyes.

I blessed him, I blessed myself, but the pain continued. I witnessed this as objectively as I could, telling myself that obviously I was still judging someone or else I would be at peace. I realized that while I didn't judge him, or myself, on very superficial levels, I was still thinking that (1) this is simply *how men behave* (no judgment there, of course!), and (2) I attract these men, which is *my* dysfunction (not exactly self-esteem). The pain I felt was like the pain of having the flu—you don't remember it until it happens again, and then you realize that you know this pain quite well. I prayed for peace.

I wanted a miracle. I wanted to live my life that day without this anxiety tearing at me.

I remembered the line that only what we are not giving can be lacking in any situation. I realized then that the problem wasn't that this man behaved a certain way; the real problem was that that particular behavior garnered my disapproval. It was not his action, but rather my own closed heart, that was causing me pain. The problem, at the deepest level, was not that he hadn't called, but that I thought that he should. What my ego had interpreted as "men always acting this way" was really just a wall they always hit, past which I wasn't willing to let them be who they were without judging them for it. Of course, they were always going to bust me on that, because the purpose of relationships is to expand us, and where our love is conditional, we need expansion.

Both people carry our wounds into a relationship. Obviously, he had his, but his issues are not my business. My own issue in this situation was unforgiveness, the limits to my capacity to accept people as they are. Most of us have places where, for whatever reason, our capacity for true forgiveness stops. The path to God, the path to our healing, is the path to our capacity for unconditional love. My love was a love that said, "I will love you—until you act this way or that way." My wounds—not just his—were clearly at issue here.

Some people would say, "But do you have to date someone who says they're going to call, and then doesn't?" Absolutely not. The point is, until I can forgive that kind of behavior, I will always be encountering it. Forgiveness doesn't mean I won't have the ability to make choices or own my own power; it just means I can make my decisions freely, without blame or anxiety. Such a position is in fact a thousand times more powerful than anger.

Clearly, I said to myself, I need to get over this man. I remember saying to a girlfriend, "He's not available for the experience." But then I heard myself say, "Oh yeah? Who's not available here?" If I had shared what I thought was love with this man, then from a spiritual perspective, the love is not determined by whether he does or does not call. Love is content and not form. His behavior is not what defines our love. As long as we are setting the agenda for someone else's behavior, then we are seeking to be their jailer, not their lover, and we will not know peace.

If our emotional stability is based on what other people do or do not do, then we have no stability. If our emotional stability is based on love that is changeless and unalterable, then we attain the stability of God. "Release him, Marianne," I said to myself. "All minds are joined, and he can feel, if only subconsciously, this pressure to be who I want him to be. Get off his case."

I had been asking God to free me of my attachment to this man, but I began to realize that God couldn't free me of what I wouldn't let go. As my friend Mary Manin Morrissey says, "God can only do for us what He can do through us." God gives us His strength by giving us His vision of things. Our seeing people as innocent is the only way to achieve God's peace.

As long as I was holding onto the thought, "If he loves me, he'll call," then I was insidiously judging him if he did not, and thus I was vulnerable to pain. To say I forgave him for not calling meant nothing as long as I was judging him for not calling in the first place! A miracle is a shift in perception from fear to love, and I made that shift, saying, "I have my experience of the connection between us. That connection is impervious to whether or not he ever gets back to me on the physical plane." I owned what was mine to own, I enjoyed what was mine to enjoy, and by the time he called, I was light as air.

❦

Dear God,
Please remove from me
my temptation to try to control another person.
I surrender this relationship
into the hands of divine spirit.
May it be blessed,
may it be sweet,
may it be free of my unforgiveness.
Amen

❦

So deep relationships are messy, they are uncomfortable, they are work; we are forced to confront those places in ourselves where we can't always practice yet what we know enough to preach. A safe lover is someone who understands that we're trying, and doesn't punish us for falling short. A dangerous lover is one who either knowingly puts his or her foot in your way so you're bound to trip over it, or tells you what a klutz you are when you trip over that foot or someone else's. Those people are not partners in an enchanted journey;

they're our partners in hell. We're absolutely right to walk away from those situations; they do not serve. The fact that we forgive someone does not mean that we can never leave that person. If anything, we can leave more easily the situations where we know in our hearts it is best to leave. To travel with God is to travel lightly.

Low-level, neurotic relationship dramas do not support our own, or the planet's, movement in the direction of God. Their prevailing characteristic is the way they always circle back upon themselves; the pain of the relationship never seems to get ultimately resolved. In that case, although one can certainly understand why Spirit would have led you to reveal each other's deepest wounds, it doesn't appear as though, at this point anyway, one or both people are ready to turn a wound into a sacred wound and make the relationship a holy environment. In those relationships, there is more judgment than forgiveness, more attack than sharing, more defensiveness than taking of personal responsibility. Hanging around for an endless repetition of the same cycle is not loving, but merely dysfunctional.

A woman once told me she was upset because her boyfriend had failed to acknowledge her birthday. My question to her was this: "Did he *forget* your birthday, or did he *ignore* your birthday?" If he just forgot it, then there are a mil-

6

lion ways that an apology and a little effort on his part could make the pain go away. But if he ignored her birthday, even passively, as though to let her know that no expectations of any kind would be tolerated here, then he is not just forgetful, he is unkind. And kindness should be a minimum standard.

God offers us, in our relationships, the perfect opportunities for maximal learning, but whether or not we choose to take advantage of those opportunities is completely up to us. A holy relationship is one in which both people understand the cosmic game that's being played here: "Hi, my weaknesses see your weaknesses. Want to dance and grow strong together?" If there is not that conscious context, that sacred environment for the issues which emerge, then unconsciousness—and ultimately pain—will dominate our interactions with the one we love. Then, no matter how romantic it had been, how great the sex or how lovely the smiles, it will all go down in burning flames and we will not be transformed. We will merely be burned.

It's helpful, when we're trying to forgive, to remember that she's known as much pain as you have known, he's as scared as you are, and no one here is perfect. Both people knowing that, in a conscious moment of shared compassion, doesn't mean our boundaries are leaky, but only that our hearts are open. We can turn this deeper acceptance of each other into a disciplined compassion. Until we do that, we will always be tempted to attack, and whenever we attack another, we are actually attacking ourselves. I remember saying to someone once, "To attack *me* is to attack *us*."

There is, inside all our heads, the ego's rabid attack dog. It is purely vicious toward others and toward ourselves as well. Learning to control that dog, and ultimately to end its life, is the process and purpose of enlightened relationships.

No one brings out the attack dog faster than the person we have chosen to love. You remind me of one of my parents; therefore, psychically, I must kill you off. You remind me of someone else who loved me, but then they humiliated me; therefore, psychically, I must kill you off. You will probably laugh at me once you really know me; therefore, psychically, I must kill you off.

What an angry generation we have been. What walls we built around the moat we dug around the fortress we constructed around our wounded hearts. And even when our prayers were answered and some sweet prince made his way past the wall, beyond the moat, through the fortress, and almost into our hearts, we sent whatever sentries necessary to shoot an arrow right into him and stop him short of his intended goal. Our slogan in love became, "Man the walls!"

But there's a mass exodus now, from behind the castle walls. Rapunzel's prince did fall from the tower and go blind, Rapunzel did lose her long hair and spend years in exile, but ultimately they refound each other. Her tears on his eyes gave him back his sight, and they lived happily ever after, after all. That's the part of the story we can witness to now, that our tears might turn into balms with which we heal each other and comfort each other, after so many years of getting it all so wrong.

&

Okay, so I have a gift for you. It is a necklace of flowers. One is the flower of forgiveness, two is the flower of my understanding, and three is the flower of my challenge to you.

What challenge, you ask? To show yourself to me. But will you still want me then? Oh yes I will, and I will love you even more.

&

Try this: Agree, as a couple, to write each other a letter. In the letters, reveal your deepest personal fears, about your life and about your relationship. Write the letters sitting next to each other, perhaps, or at least at the same general time. When you exchange the letters, agree *not to read them.* The ritual is to say, "I am willing to hold your fears, to be a space for the miracle which obliterates them. But I will not go too far, I will not put my fingers on an open wound, I will not look at what you are not ready for me to see, or hear what you would prefer I not know." And then the risk: Agree to put the letter from your beloved somewhere important and sacred, yet leave it unread. Perhaps create an altar just for your love, a clean and beautiful place in your home where you dedicate thoughts and things to the furtherance of the sacred bond between you.

And then, one night or one morning, when the growing intimacy between you is making each of you feel more safe and courageous, one of you will say, "You can read my letter now." Or perhaps you will read your own, out loud. But you should pray first, asking God to handle this, surrendering to Him your fears, and your lover's fears, and your reactions to each other.

"Help me, dear God, to see my loved one's innocence, and please help him (or her) see mine. As we admit our weaknesses, make us strong. As we admit our fears, make our love grow deeper." Kiss again, before you open the letters. Then the magic will emerge, taking your words and turning them into medicine. Your vulnerability, then, will bless your love, when before it might have hurt it.

We all make mistakes, we all have fears, and we all have weaknesses. *Behind* all that is our essential self. When our essential self has made contact with another, the light is dazzling and would fill the universe. The challenge of enchantment is to remain faithful to that light, to believe in it even when it is not so apparent. Then that light becomes an incandescent glow and it wraps itself around everything. The mundane begins to sparkle, not just for a few weeks, or even for a year, but for a lifetime and beyond.

It takes devotion to invoke and maintain the light of romance. It takes the practice of forgiveness on the deepest level, the intention to focus on our beloved's innocence, even when it's not showing. And when that light is covered over by clouds, when he said or she said or he did or she did not, there is a deeper truth than is revealed by these machinations of someone's personality self. The power lies in just *knowing* this, in being still and *knowing*, in being willing to let go everything except the absolute and committed knowledge that the love that you have touched in each other, and the light that it revealed, was real, is real, and shall always be real.

Sometimes we find ourselves in horrible fights, and a part of us says, "This can't be real!" We think that because it is true. The fight between you is not real. Only love exists on an indestructible cosmic level. Just knowing that creates the space for a miracle to happen.

The miracle could be that two people who had been struggling and arguing just moments before now look at each other and begin to laugh. Or it might mean that one or both of you sadly, but lovingly, realizes it's time to part, that physical proximity no longer serves your mutual growth. The enchanted issue is not whether bodies stay together or not, but whether hearts and minds are reconciled. In God's world, content is more important than form. In the world as it is now, form is everything and content practically nothing. That is why it hurts here. That is why it is time to move on to something better.

And God has graced us with a way.

Dear God,
We surrender this relationship to You
and ask that it be used for Your purposes.
May our resources and talents
and energies and love
be pooled
and lifted up in Your service.
May we become together
even more than we are apart.
May the light around us
forever shine.
May the space of our love
be a space of healing
for ourselves and all the world.
Amen

8

⚘

Partnership

*I cannot get to sleep without my leg wrapped around yours.
I cannot stay awake without my brain wrapped around
yours. I cannot get to heaven without my heart wrapped
around yours.*

So there! Have I revealed enough . . . ?

⚘

SOMETIMES ANOTHER PERSON'S energy can
feel like excess baggage we can't afford to carry. It's as
though we're trying to lift a plane, and too much
weight just isn't an option during take-off.

Once the plane is in the sky, however, the situation can seem to change dramatically. Where it felt before like we couldn't take off if another person was weighing us down, it now begins to feel as though holding a plane in the sky is too big a job for just one person.

And that's what partners are: two people carrying the same load, two wings on the same plane, two people doing a job that is just too big for one person to do alone. The planet is being bombarded with powerful energy today; people are being given tasks too big, not so much for our physical selves to carry alone, as for one consciousness to carry alone. We need partners to share the emotional and spiritual burdens of our lives, at a time when life itself is being transformed at the very deepest levels. Sometimes you can do all the physical work by yourself, or hire or find others to help you complete it. But at the end of the day, how we long for someone to *understand* it all with us! When there is mischievous laughter to laugh, or painful tears to cry, we long to do that with someone who truly understands the depth of both our laughter and our tears.

If you're very, very lucky, you have had the experience of being one of two hearts beating in what feels like the same as-tral body. You use your eyes, and he uses his eyes, but really there is only one being here, with two different bodies to provide optimum functioning in the physical world. Physical separation is experienced, in this situation, as the fantasy and illusion that, in cosmic terms, it actually is. This is an exhilarating space, a sometimes terrifying space, because it is a field beyond the body. The world of enchanted partnership is a whole new world indeed.

Enchantment is not just a facet of romance, but of a new, emerging planetary consciousness. It is the psychic womb out of which will be born a new humanity. Enchanted partnerships produce enchanted environments, and children who grow up in enchanted environments will forever bear the mark of its magic. They will in turn recreate the world. They will explode the myths of former times. They will receive the inheritance of our endless wealth, of love and satisfaction and peace immeasurable. Their hearts will dilate, and their genes will be altered by an outpouring of spiritual light. They will sing what we sing and they will know what we know. And even when their minds forget, their hearts will always remember.

&

I've been swimming all my life, you said, but I never saw these things. Ah, you swam, but never before without the fear of drowning. Lie back, and I will swim you home. The stars will guide us, the waves will carry us, and all our fear will slip away. Surrender now. The sea caresses. Together we will meet the sky, and find our love for everything.

෴

To yield to love is to yield to an emptiness from which there is always a sense that we might not return. It takes faith and confidence to surrender so, to an ocean that might not hold you.

Enchantment impels us to leave old ground behind; where we have been no longer feeds us, but rather threatens to destroy us. Living only on dry land constricts our spirits and dries up our juices. Life is leading us back to sea.

Enchanted lovers do not conform to the status quo of boredom, or routine, or passionless existence. They have tasted for a moment another possibility, and while the majority of couples allow the world to whittle away at their joy and freedom, more and more now say, "Let's stay in this light. Let's not go back." Let's not go back to what we *have* to do; from here on out, let's commit to the drama of ecstatic joining, and to its endless possibilities for expansion. At a certain point, no more outer growth is possible until more inner growth occurs. And this inner growth takes concerted effort; it takes all our spiritual, psychological, emotional, and even intellectual prowess to create and maintain the space of our enchantment, but the effort will make the stars in the sky even brighter. Blessings pour forth when we join hands with another and say, "In our world, at least, though we will see the demons, we will take them on. In our world, at least, though we will feel our weaknesses, we will work to transform them. In our world, at least, though we face a world that looks bitterly on love, and lovingly on guilt, we will commit to each other's innocence."

As that commitment begins to permeate our consciousness, a crown floats down from the firmaments of heaven and is placed on both our heads. With that crown is given us dominion over all things fearful, a power with which to rule our inner worlds and outer kingdoms, providing for ourselves and others a new possibility for peace on earth.

Turn to your loved one and ask yourself, "Is this my partner in a grand and passionate, sacred romantic adventure?" Your heart will say yes or your heart will say no. If the answer is yes, then within yourself, fall to your knees and thank God.

If the answer is no, then ask the spirit of God to reveal to you now where you should go and what you should do to find your enchanted love. Then wait with a grateful heart, an alert mind, and a joyful knowing. Around each corner there are miracles. Around each bend await more angels. Around midnight, they will come and you will know.

∾

IN EVERY HEART there is an inner room, where we hold our greatest treasures and our deepest pain. We hold the skeletons of our former selves, our childhood fears and insecurities, and terror at our dissociation from God's forgiveness and love. We have built our lives not so much on the foundation of God's love as on our best efforts to function in spite of its absence. We stumble into adulthood as broken beings, many of us, carrying the wounds of childhood on our hearts like invisible scars. Contagion seeps from the broken psychic flesh of our battered places, expressed less as vulnerable tears than as angry shrieks, until we have done our inner work. Until then, others do not feel our pain, so much as the pain we inflict on *them* because of it. And the cycle of suffering turns another rotation, inflicting men, women, and children with fears that will, if unchecked, destroy the world.

Therapy, spiritual practice, prayer, meditation, men's groups, women's groups, seminars, retreats, alone time, tears, writing letters, doing ritual, processing with friends, sweat lodges, healing techniques, going to church, going to synagogue, going to the ashram, going to the mosque, attending support groups, doing the twelve steps, burning incense, making lists, making amends, journaling, doing service, creative visualization, saying affirmations—God knows they all help, and by now, God knows we've done them all. But there's something altogether different that happens when the one you love stands before you and says, "I will descend into the fire with you, and come out on the other side. I see it all and I can take it all. I love it all. Let's hunker down and do the work together."

There comes a point where we have done as much of the inner work as we can do by ourselves. For a long time, many of us felt the need to forgo intimate relationships while we did our inner work, from which those dramas distracted us. But the emotional *zeitgeist* has shifted now; at this point, we need intimate relationships *in order to go further* with our inner work. Intimacy has become our new frontier because honesty

in life is relatively easy, while honesty with an intimate partner is ten times harder; integrity in life is relatively easy, while
integrity regarding an intimate partner is a much more con-
fusing issue; and forgiveness as a principle is easy enough to
grasp, while forgiving an intimate partner can take more wisdom and grace than we feel we're capable of.

To commit to the dynamics of an enchanted romance is to
commit to climbing an emotional mountain, embarking together on a potentially perilous journey. It is to say, "What
we know of relationship dramas is not what we want now.
Our prayer is to not repeat the past. We invite the spirit of
God to enter this relationship with us, to transform the
thoughts we carry from before, to open our eyes to the awesome vision that stands before us now, to help us not cower in
fear before the beauty and the power that we see in each other.
May the potential of this love become its reality." On earth,
as it is in heaven. And during the day, as during the night.

℮ↄ

MY GENERATION paid a terrible price for our overcasual-
ization of romance, particularly its sexual element. It is as
though we toyed with the emotional equivalent of nuclear

power, and upon realizing this, have now created the sexual equivalent of the anti-nuclear movement. We don't want to get rid of sex, but neither do we want sex to get rid of us! We are looking for new containers for the power unleashed when two hearts recognize each other and in their excitement collide. The answer to our former destructiveness is not to avoid romantic love but to recreate it. We need new models for romantic expression in an age when we are ready at last to be truly mature, and know that spiritual perspective is the hallmark of maturity.

We have not put romance and sex in the same category as God and spiritual practice for a very long time, if ever. The most we have been able to do is find ancient traditions, usually not even from our own cultural or religious lineages, that delineate possibilities for grace-filled romantic experiences. But it is time for our generation of Westerners to claim for ourselves, in the context of our own traditions, the notion of holy romance in today's astounding world. In both Judaism and Christianity, the communication has been mainly, "Get married, and then we'll talk." Well, *hello.* What if we're not married? Does that mean that there is nothing spiritual in our relationships to work on until then?

The spiritual crux of romance is the issue of partnership

itself: Am I going through this life alone, or am I walking with my beloved? Are we competitors, or are we allies? Are we two parallel tracks, or are we entwined? Are we parallel in some ways, and entwined in others? Are we parallel on some days, and entwined on others? Which day is which? And do we know how we truly feel about these things, and do we know how our partner feels?

These issues demand serious and heartfelt conversation of a kind that doesn't just happen by itself. Yet it is depth of conversation and forgiveness, not the joining of bodies, that determines the presence or absence of real relationship. Until we know this, there is a level on which we are bound to emotionally walk alone, even if our bodies sleep with the same person for twenty or thirty years. What is the goal of our relationship? That is the question we ultimately face. Is the goal to have a warm body next to us (decent goal, but not necessarily magical)? Is the goal to raise children (decent goal, but not necessarily magical)? Is the goal to create a home together (decent goal, but not necessarily magical)? Or is the goal to find an enchanted realm of ever-expanding opportunities, for growth of who we are and who we can be together, lighting both our inner and our outer skies? *Then* sex is magical; *then* raising children is magical; *then* a home is magical.

If we want enchantment, we have to prepare the brew. And that takes effort, as writing a song takes effort or building a house takes effort. It takes inner as well as outer work: dedication to the discernment of spiritual truth as it flows through our lives and relationships, learning the ways of forgiveness, authentically and compassionately, what it means to show up for another person, what it means to give something from the depths of ourselves, what it means to receive, what it means to make another person feel safe without indulging his or her neuroses, what it means to take responsibility for our own issues, what it means to bless and support someone else, what it means to meditate with another, to pray with another, to reveal to another, to delight another, to celebrate another, to create new life on some level with another, to avoid the temptation to abandon another, to avoid the temptation to attack another, to learn to be kind and patient even when we're not at all in the mood, and still—in the midst of it all—to NOT rely on another for either our sustenance or our wholeness. To remember always that God is here, in the middle of the relationship, and that what your beloved cannot give you today, God gives you always.

When we master any of those energies, for an hour or even for a moment, we transcend emotional gravity. We move into a realm not of infatuation but of heightened reality, a very serious emotional and spiritual flow that, when achieved by enough of us, will cut like a laser through the encrusted darkness of the world, remove the rock, resurrect our lives, and start the world all over again.

❧

"Your reality is so different than mine," you said.

"How so?" I asked.

"The way you see the relationship is so much more mystical than the way I see it."

"I don't know if I buy that," I said. "I couldn't be seeing what I'm seeing unless you were seeing it too."

"That's true," you said.

"In fact, to be honest, I think you're a closet mystic."

"True as stated," you said.

"So isn't there an issue here about owning who you really are? Have you heard the story about the eagle and the chickens, where the baby eagle got raised by chickens so no one told him he had wings?"

"Yes," you said. "I have. Joseph Campbell told an even better one. A mother lion, heavy with child, threw herself into a herd of lambs, to

feed. But she was so heavy that the fall killed her. The baby lion was born, and then was raised among the lambs.

"*After a passage of time, a male lion was preparing to attack the lambs in order to feed. All of a sudden, he saw a young lion among them, and said, 'What are you doing here?'*

" *'Ba-a-a-h,' was the young lion's response.*

"*So the adult lion took the young lion aside, telling him who he was and forcing him to eat the meat that lions are supposed to eat. The young lion gagged at first, and had a hard time swallowing it. But in the end he came to realize that this was his food, and this was his leonine nature.*"

The story obviously meant a lot to you. I could tell by the way you sighed. And later I realized it was my story, too. I'm the reverse tale: I am a lamb who was raised among lions. We are both trying to actualize our own essential natures now, and recognize in each other a spiritual mentor. You feel good when you're around me because, in my presence, you feel like a lion. And I feel good when I'm around you, because in your presence I feel like a lamb.

Out of your wound came the medicine for my healing, and out of my wound came the medicine for yours. God, in His infinite mercy and genius, uses even the darkness to create more light.

At the highest level of our being, the lion lies down with the lamb. Our strength and our gentleness, our assertiveness and our tender-

ness, our male and our female, our leader and our follower, our yin and our yang, our divinity and our humanity, all merge together in harmony and balance.

And then, when the universe is really sparkling . . . you lie down with me.

∾

My friend Sandy Scott says that every relationship involves a "gift exchange." There's always an exchange of gifts in a relationship, and knowing this reminds us of the spiritual purpose of having one. There are lessons for us to teach, and lessons for us to learn, in every human encounter.

In intimacy, our capacity to love is the greatest, and our temptation to judge is the greatest as well. The possibility that we will merge our heart with the heart of another is the negative ego's greatest fear, because that merger is the death of the ego! Fear-based ego is nothing more than the *belief* that we are separate beings, and truly joining with another puts the lie to that lie. It is the crucifix in front of the vampire, the casting out of devils, the water Dorothy poured over the Wicked Witch, the kiss of the prince, and the resurrection of our divine nature.

Once we have experienced true joining with anyone, then the track is laid for our minds to experience it with everyone. That doesn't mean we will, but it means we have an increased emotional capacity for doing so. A softened heart toward anyone makes the heart at least potentially softer in its dealings with the world. Intimate love is spiritual training for everything in life. It is not meant to be an exclusive sanctuary from the pain of the world, but rather an inclusive balm for the sorrows of the world. In learning to show up more fully for one person, we learn to show up more fully for the life.

It always blows me away when people say they "don't have time" for a relationship. And what else is time for? For what other purpose are we living our lives? And can we really be passionate and creative in one area while we suppress our passion and creativity somewhere else? Emotion is like water. It can't be cut down the middle. It can't be put on a shelf. Intimate love, particularly an enchanted love, is the engine room for a certain kind of creative existence. When the burners are blasting there, the entire ship is ablaze with magic.

It is a broader, more universal love toward which the planet is evolving, and all individual relationships are meant to serve that higher purpose. That is why there is such cosmic momentum behind true romance. It feels, when we fall in love, as though we have received a gift from God, and in fact we have. But when God gives a gift to anyone, it is never meant for that person alone. All gifts of God are intended for everyone. Spirit recognizes that in a particular combination of souls, the highest possibilities exist for the evolution of all living beings. Spirit sent Jennifer to John because, within this love, she has more chance of becoming, and more quickly, the woman she is capable of being. And Spirit sent John to Jennifer for exactly the same reason. Spirit thus gave both John and Jennifer to one another as their relationship "assignment." In that sense, Cupid is very real indeed. His arrow says, "Stop and look at this person. There is something for you to learn here, and something for you to teach."

And God's gifts never stop giving. If Jennifer is lifted, and John is lifted, then the *world* is lifted in ways that neither of them will ever even know. As Jennifer and John are lifted *together,* then their gifts to the world are exponentially increased. That is why people cry at weddings. We're not just happy for the lucky couple; rather, we unconsciously know that if this depth of devotion is possible for anyone, then it's possible on some level for all of us.

When two hearts join in ecstasy and rapture, an army of light ascends and the world is brought closer to heaven. *Liter-*

ally. The beloved's hand on us, like a baby's hand, holds a power that is straight from God. Heaven is, in metaphysical terms, the experience of our oneness. The world is a holographic universe, with every piece containing the whole. An enchanted love between any two people is a blessing on the entire world.

Thus the awesome power and responsibility of intimacy. The question that faces us is so much deeper than, "Are my needs being met here?" It becomes, "How can the world be blessed by our having found each other?" God wants us to be deeply, completely, and powerfully happy, because happy people are the most effective people. If your partner left the house feeling happier this morning because he or she spent the night with you, then know this: you served the world today. Just *being* in a good relationship is an ultimate service to the planet.

And yet, for all its obvious magic, love is as daunting at times as it is compelling. The deeper our fear of the light at the center of ourselves, the deeper our fear of truly loving another. No matter how much a relationship blesses us, no matter how good it feels, and even perhaps at times *because* it feels so good, this soul medicine, when first offered up, can appear to the mind like a cup of poison. Enchanted partnership takes courage, because it challenges us to *be*. In the words of Elizabeth Barrett Browning, "God answers sharp and sudden on some prayers, and thrusts the thing we have prayed for in our face, a gauntlet with a gift in it." God brings us love, but we must meet it with courage or it will slip through our hands. When love walks in, we had best meet it with backbone.

And when we do, we become different creatures. We are no longer adrift in our own aloneness, but are anchored in a steady love. Our ship is sturdy. Our love is to be depended on—not because its form will never change, but because someone else has given us their promise, with their eyes, with their actions, with their words, with their kisses, that this bond is neither small nor unimportant, that this commitment shall in some way last forever, and this lifetime shall not be lived alone.

ↄ

"I thought you would never get here," I said.
"I know. And that's what took me so long. . . ."

ↄ

Dear God,
Please lift my heart
above the pain
of former trials.
Remove from me
the thoughts
that hold me back.
Make clean my heart,
make clear my mind,
make new my life.
Amen

9

❧

Removing the Ghosts

There are monsters in my past, my darling.

So what? I have a few in mine. But I am not the monster.

I am not the monster, and the monster is not me.

❧

FROM THE PERSPECTIVE of miracles, only love is real. Nothing else exists. The fact that something is in cosmic terms mere illusion, however, doesn't mean it doesn't have the power, if left unhealed, to ruin your life. In this physical world, illusions are very powerful indeed.

One of the places where we all tend to hold the greatest amount of unhealed fear is in our relationships with our parents, and until that fear is downloaded from our psyches, we tend to carry it like baggage into our adult relationships. Forgiving our parents is imperative if we want a healed, enchanted love.

Many of us carry deep and serious wounds from childhood. Child abuse and neglect abound in the United States and have for years. They are played out in various forms of spiritual, mental, emotional, and physical violation, and literally millions of Americans are the seriously walking wounded.

Others of us are not the seriously walking wounded—we did not suffer at the hands of seriously pathological parents—but nevertheless we are the walking wounded still, having been brought up by people just like us, parents who tried their best but could not help but pass on the wounds that they themselves received as children.

For years I couldn't figure out how much of our past, particularly family issues, we had to delve into in our efforts to emotionally heal ourselves. I knew that most of us carry scars from childhood, but I saw so many people overindulge themselves harping on it. Living in the past can be merely an excuse to avoid the present. More than anything, I was afraid that were I to look too closely into my past, I might end up judging someone I didn't want to judge or blaming someone I don't want to blame. The last thing I wanted to be was someone blaming all my problems on my parents.

Yet looking with spiritual perspective at our childhood issues doesn't lead us, in the end, to blame others, but rather to simply understand them more deeply. Until we do that, it can be hard to unravel the personal mysteries that limit our awareness. Unresolved childhood dramas can be very disempowering. They create and maintain the fear-based, unrecognized beliefs that run our lives without our knowing it. And they can limit our capacity to forgive by limiting our ability to understand who and what it is that we need to forgive.

To say "I don't blame my parents" is not necessarily the same thing as saying, "I hold them blameless." Saying that you don't blame your parents can be just a disguise for saying, "I do blame them, but I don't want to have to admit the fact that I'm judgmental!" Real forgiveness is when you realize that in the larger scheme of things there's nothing to forgive, because all mistakes are a call for love, and lovelessness has no permanent effect. But spiritual work is not a substitute for psychological work. And forgiving someone can be much easier to do when you have a fuller understanding of his or her life experience.

Our parents had parents, too—they were wounded as children, too—and they didn't know any more about how to get it right in this life than we do. Most of us are not victims of our parents, so much as we *and* our parents have all been living for years at the effect of the unevolved, fear-based energies permeating this world. None of us deserves blame and all of us deserve compassion. Sometimes you can't really forgive your parents until you have allowed yourself to cry for them.

I was raised, like millions of others around my age, by the "tumbler generation." Almost every night when my father got home from work, he would drink a highball, one jigger of scotch with water. No one at that time would have considered this anything other than simple relaxation. He was certainly not a drunk, not as we think of that term. But what I understand now is that that one drink every night when my father got home was just enough buffer between him and his own emotions to guarantee that he would not be available to mine. I grew up starved for a certain emotional closeness with my father, and later in life would set up man after man to be as abstractly adoring as my father was abstractly adoring, yet ultimately as emotionally detached as my father was emotionally detached.

My father always seemed uncomfortable with the intensity of my feeling nature, and I grew up constantly trying too hard to get from him what I would never get, no matter what. That intensity became like a black mark on my personality. Like many people who grew up in emotional circumstances similar to mine, I developed a river of anger in the background of my psyche—anger at my father, though I didn't know that for years. I set men up to withhold from me—or at least I interpreted their behavior as such—and then projected onto them the anger I really felt toward my father, for never having given me the emotional sustenance I craved. Some poor guy wouldn't even know what had hit him, when all of a sudden he was being demanded psychological payment for something that Daddy did or didn't do, twenty years before.

Ultimately, when I began to look into the conditions of my father's own childhood—the kind of parents he had, the poverty and hardships that his family endured—I began to see his personality in a different way. And having your own children helps, of course, because you start considering that the parent you've been blaming probably did better at this job than you're doing! I let go my anger at my father for what I felt he had not given me, taking responsibility for my own unconsciousness in projecting so much blame onto him. I let myself experience the true respect and love I feel for my father, for his having created the amazing life he did out of the emotionally damaging circumstances of his own life. Then I could appreciate all the ways he *was* there for me, that he did try to be available to me as a father and did provide me with incredible gifts on many, many levels. And as the years went by, he himself went through many changes and became a more emotionally present man. But I had to realize the dark before I could truly embrace the light. Then I could begin to feel compassion for his pain as well as mine, and I began to recognize the work *I* had to do, to clean up my emotional responses toward him and toward other men, as well.

So many of us carry around the dead bodies of former aspects of ourselves, dimensions of joy that got shut down years ago and never breathed again. I actually remember my birth, I think. I remember coming out and seeing the light above the operating table, shining so bright in the new world where I'd just arrived. Like every newborn baby, I came carrying an awesome love for the world, ready to give this gift I had carried straight from the heart of God. But then, something happened. A man—the doctor, of course—*hit* me! And although my mother's doctor honestly thought that that was the way to make me breathe, of course, my total shock and horror that someone would hurt me blasted me into a dimension of darkness from which I don't think I have ever fully escaped.

But what I know now about that doctor is what I know about my father: He didn't know any better. He didn't mean to hurt me. He didn't mean to violate anyone. He, like you and I today, was doing the best he knew how to do. These men were certainly not bad. Like us, they were trying. Like us, they stumbled. And like us, they tried their best to get up, whenever they could see that there was an error in their ways.

When my father died, I felt he came to me. I felt his soul say to me, "Oh, *that's* who you are. Littlest Sister, I'm so sorry. I will be there for you now. I promise." And I feel in my heart that he has been, and he is.

If anyone is a victim, my father was, more than I am. He lived in a world, and in a family, where genuine emotion was practically outlawed. It was stuffed before it had a chance to emerge. No wonder he fathered an emotional volcano; I was doomed to carry the emotional baggage that neither of my parents was owning. How else is the world going to right itself, except through children who have no choice but to unconsciously rebel against painful patterns in a family's past?

And my daughter will do the same with me. I hope she will heal any wounds inflicted on her by my unconsciousness, but I also know that the greatest gift I can give her is to heal my own wounds as best I can, now. I don't want my daughter to spend years in therapy trying to heal from her relationship with me. I want her to see her mother get it right. And that is what forgiveness has helped me do.

Until I could see my father's pain, I was narcissistically wrapped up in my own. And as long as that was true, I was too immature to have any sense of the pain of a man who was in my arms. While my father's pain was invisible to me, all men's pain was invisible to me. My own took up the entire screen.

No one knows how to love who has no tenderness or mercy toward the wounded heart of another. As the love of God began to free me from my past, and heal the wounds of my violent heart, I began to see men through vastly different eyes. Forgiving the men in my past became fairly easy to do, once I recognized my own neurotic behavior and how it had contributed to theirs. What had formerly made me cry began to make me laugh.

I learned years ago that only what we are not giving can be lacking in any situation. I withheld respect from men, at the deepest, most insidious levels. But respect was not so hard to give to men, once I realized that they have their own pain, and my seeing my father's was the key to that. I saw how deeply men are violated in this civilization, every bit as much as women. They deserve respect for the fact that they continue to try to find strength and courage in a world that allows them so little permission to express their feelings. Women's emotions are often made to appear foolish, but men's emotions are hardly allowed at all. Holding a little boy, it's so clear they're no different when they cry than little girls are. They're no less sensitive and no less needing of love. Some people will read this, of course, and say, "Duh." But, I admit to you, for me that was a revelation.

If you are not sensitive to your own suffering, you lack the capacity to be sensitive to the pain in someone else. It is not to our discredit that we have suffered; it is to our credit that we have suffered and then risen back up. And whether our consciousness of arousal is Isis lifting up Osiris from the dead, or Jesus resurrecting, or tears in our eyes at the first sign of spring, or falling in love when it seemed it would never happen again, or forgiving when it had seemed we were too damaged to forgive, God has a way of shining a light on all the darkness of the past and releasing us to a light-filled present. Once we have started to forgive the past, we can begin to forgive the present. And in forgiving the present, we reprogram the future. Forgiveness can become a mental habit, a disciplined and continuous effort to see the innocence in other people. Then we have the power to exorcise the emotional ghosts that will otherwise haunt us forever.

We are often so hurt by what happened in the past that we are afraid to allow the present to just *be*. We project onto someone now standing in front of us the mistakes of someone we haven't seen for years. We falsely believe that judging someone now will somehow give us more power or control over our destiny. The opposite of course is true, because *judgment is the death of enchantment.* And if we're living in judgment, then we are bound to be judged!

Judgment remains our most prevalent disease, and it's often doled out disguised as medicine. Girlfriends, even so-called healers, sit around and talk. "Don't let him do this," we say. "This is a bad sign. I've seen him do that before. He's not treating you right." It's all an unconscious game of "Let me reject you before you have a chance to reject me." In fact, running the present through the filter of the past just dooms us to repeat it. If we're trying to compensate for a former lack, then our core belief is lack, not plenty. And that is what we will recreate.

It takes conscious effort to focus on *what people do right.* "Yes, but that's not *reality*," some people say—as though guilt is some major reality and innocence is just mere fiction.

Finally we wake up and realize, "What the hell am I doing? Am I without sin? Am I without faults? Am I without mistakes? Do I prefer that people focus on what I do wrong, or on my efforts to do right?" People who choose not to condemn us are not our enablers but our healers. What do we choose to be to others? Attacking people hardly increases their capacity to learn from us.

And since we're not perfect, why would anyone else be? It's going to be a long, long wait if we're waiting for that perfect person, because perfect people don't exist.

One of my girlfriends used to say to me, "I can only be with a man so long before I start to think that everything he does is wrong." How familiar. For a week and a half, the beloved is so delightful. And then the darkness sets in, not in them but in us. We start to judge whatever they do—when they call, when they don't, what they say, what they don't. The ego has been alerted: Two souls have made contact here, and might actually join their hearts. Next thing you know, they'll be seeing each other as sinless, experiencing the love of God. *And that would mean the death of the ego.* All heaven would break loose. Can't have that, the ego says. Send out the scavenger dogs, and bring home the guilt, the guilt, the guilt, the guilt, the guilt.

I am not suggesting that we not have principles, or standards, or feelings in our guts that we listen to and heed. In fact, those are all important. But I have noticed—in myself and others—an automatic projection of shame and guilt onto those we had previously thought so wonderful, which is less about the other person and more about our own investment in guilt, sucked to the surface in the presence of love. We've heard the line, "Love brings up everything unlike itself." Fear is detoxed, subconsciously brought to the fore whenever love arrives. Once aroused, it will either trigger us or depart from us, depending on whether it is forgiven or punished. Forgiveness is the hottest topic in love right now, because without it there is no love.

We all have romantic projections that fill our minds, fed by movies and media and stories of other people's lives that seem

more important than our own. It seems as though those stories are enchanted, while the actual lover in front of us is not.
This is such a hideous distortion, because the opposite is the
truth. These projections can be deadly. They do not honor
real life. The person we love, on the other hand, has all the
makings of a mythical character, if we would learn to
mythologize rather than pathologize love.

As with illness and death, there are all these voices of
pseudo-wisdom in our society today, screeching "Denial!"
whenever anyone has the audacity to proclaim a higher
ground to live on. "No, I do not choose to accept that this
disease is necessarily terminal. There are always cases of re-
mission." "*Denial!*" they yell. "No, I do not choose to focus on
what he did wrong here. I want to focus on the things he did
right." "*Denial!*" they yell. I say, denial, schmenial. To deny the
power of error to hurt the child of God is not negative denial
but spiritual power.

There *are* goddesses and queens within every woman; we're
not crazy to think that. There *are* gods and kings within every
man; we're not crazy to think that. What this world calls realism is a distorted picture of God's reality. Rose-colored
glasses are not the worst things we can put on, because at
times they can actually help us see.

Enchantment, like holiness, dwells beyond the veil. It is a world that arises when we extend our perceptions beyond what the body's eyes reveal. We choose to look past personality to a sweeter, more peaceful reality on the other side. There we find a deeper, more creative love. It is a choice, a decision, that takes us there. It is an adult rite of passage to reach out for this dimension, and claim it for our own. We consciously prepare ourselves for enchantment; even then, it isn't brought to us but merely offered to us, and it is absolutely our choice whether or not to enter its sacred realms.

Whether the beloved is a person or still yet just a thought, we should bless his or her path to our door.

❧

Dear God,
I pray today for the one I love.
I pray to see her tenderness,
I pray to see her innocence,
and I pray that she'll see mine.
I pray that she be surrounded by light,
that Your angels come and bless her.
I pray that she'll be happy,

and her heart be filled with love.
I pray that I might be to her
a man who honors and adores her.
Her gladdened heart is joy to me.
Thank you, God.
Amen

ↇↄ

The ego sees people as they *were* and not as they *are*. It is invested in the past and blind to the present. In the ego's eyes, we are doomed to the past—to who we were in the past and to our mistakes in the past. That perception is the death of innocence.

Forgiveness gives us new eyes, and with that, the capacity to give new life. That is not a metaphor, but a heightened reality. What we choose to see, we give psychic permission to appear. To say "No, I do not see you as your past, but as who you are now," is to emotionally and spiritually give someone wings. That is why, without forgiveness, the realm of enchantment is invisible. It releases us to be who we are capable of being, rather than who we showed up as before. If we're with someone who limits us to who we used to be, then the only way we can grow is to find someone who didn't *know* us before. And that, of course, can be the death knell of long-standing relationships.

From the perspective of miracles, it is our job to tell a brother he is right, even when he is wrong. That doesn't mean I'm supposed to tell you you sang a beautiful solo, when in fact your tone was flat and your notes were all over the place. It means that it's my job to make you believe in your singing ability, even when you didn't make the grade during one particular performance. Or to let you know that your worth is incalculable, even if singing isn't your forte.

In order to be romantic mystics, we must be vigilant on behalf of the beauty in all of us. That is the greatest gift that we can give one another: permission to just get better and better. In a world that seeks constantly to tear us down, isn't it wonderful to have a partner who lifts you up?

People always used to say to me, "What do you need in this relationship? What do you need in this relationship?" It became our generation's mantra. But it became clear to me that what I *needed* was to think about someone else's needs every once in a while! What all of us need, at bottom, is the same: to be free of the past, free to start over, free to feel that we're good and decent people, and free to feel there's something good and true and beautiful we can contribute to this world. Our learning how to see others that way is the greatest contribution we can make to their lives. And the person who makes us feel this way is a gift beyond rubies or gold.

〜

NONE OF US are who we were yesterday; we're certainly not who we were ten years ago. In fact, we're not even who we were five minutes ago. In every instant, we are blessed by God with the opportunity to reinvent ourselves, to transform our entire lives through grace and commitment and action and love. May we become, in our romances, as gracious to each other as God is gracious to both of us. An enchanted love is a context where we can be constantly reborn, partly because the person in front of us has no attachment to our remaining who we used to be.

I've known people who viewed changes I went through with encouragement and faith in my capacity to grow. But I have also known the types of personalities who are threatened by change. Part of an enchanted commitment is to join with another person in the thought that he or she is capable of being today someone different from the person he or she was yesterday; that we are not bound by our mistakes, as long as we try to clean them up; that God has plans for all of us, and none of those plans are less than mighty; that miracles are not only possible but also probable in our beloved's life, in part because of the holiness of our bond and the power of our agreement. Enchantment results from two people recognizing the extraordinary opportunities of love: You will not fall down today because my love is here for you. You will not be emotionally homeless today because my love is here for you. You will not be lonely today because my love is here for you. I see you in the arms of God, and I know that we are there together.

I have performed many marriage ceremonies and I know it is easy enough for people to embrace such thinking on their wedding day. But as with anything else, the tenor of our lives is not determined by our thinking on any one given day, so much as by the habitual thought patterns that dominate our daily lives. Commitment is only true if it is made again each day. Otherwise it deteriorates into little less than, "I commit to bring my body home." If you don't bring your soul home, your emotions home, your heart home, then why bother?

An enchanted love is holy ground where the meanness and the assaults of the world are not escaped so much as transformed by the power of love and forgiveness. First, I commit to forgive you, to try my best to focus on your innocence and not your errors, to bless instead of condemn you, to support instead of invalidate your efforts. I pray that God will show me who you are today, and save me from my temptation to always focus on your personality and your mistakes and your yesterdays. I wish to see you through ever new eyes. I wish to be your spiritual partner, first and foremost seeing the light in you. I wish to be my best today, that I might be worthy of this higher ground we have chosen for our love.

ॐ

MANY COUPLES demystify their intimacy, destroying the filaments of enchantment that would otherwise run like spiritual currents through it. They remove all magic in the name of mental health. It is not mental health, but spiritual laziness, to remove the mystery of love.

I was once visiting a girlfriend at her apartment in Paris. She was listening to a radio interview with great interest, and I was frustrated because I do not speak French. She seemed so intrigued by what she was hearing. When the interview was over, I asked her to tell me what she'd heard that had obviously been so interesting. She told me of a very famous French couple who have been married many, many years. The interview was with the wife. Having been asked by the radio host to reveal the secret to her long and successful marriage, the woman had responded, "I never, ever lost my mystery!"

Mystery is not a lie, but in fact a deeper level of truth. A woman's mystery is the power of Isis and Mary, a goddess field from whence flows the spiritual ability to make all things new. And men, of course, are magic too. Their love derives from the same cosmic mystery, the same divine sea as ours. To stand before each other in profound not-knowing, consciously willing to leave behind the assumptions we have carried from former, now dead moments of our lives, is to enter the mystery together. We can live our relationships from *within* the mystery that brought us to each other; then and only then can the mystery continue to unfold between us.

Isis and Osiris weren't just lovers; they were brother and sister. A problem many of us have with romance is that once someone becomes our lover, they stop being our beloved brother or sister. That is why sex too early in a relationship can be so dangerous. Spiritually, someone should clearly be our family, a truly beloved friend, before he or she becomes our lover. Sex can, and usually does, bring up every demon that lies within us. Only a sacred, loving context is a safe enough container for such an explosion of emotional force.

In every bank there is a door to a vault. Inside the vault lies gold. In each of us there is such a door, and an enchanted love is the key to unlock it. When someone truly makes the journey with you, when they try to understand your dreams, when someone truly respects your goals, when they truly hear your feelings, when someone truly stands at your side, when someone can laugh and cry with you with equal ease, when someone invites you to surrender all inhibitions and you know the invitation is safe, when someone honestly thinks you're gorgeous, when someone recognizes your bravery and salutes you for it, when someone has compassion for your wounds, when someone forgives you regularly while indulging you rarely, your molecules transform.

And therein lies the mystery of love.

Yet even then, when such a miracle happens, its light will diminish if we do not commit to its continued shining.

Lightning strikes, but we are at choice whether or not to harness the power of its electricity. We will meet who we are supposed to meet, as the meeting itself is ordained by God. But what we do with the relationship is entirely up to us. Enchanted love, under the direction of God's spirit, is both a path to and an example of divine illumination.

All who meet, according to the principles of miracles, will one day meet again until their relationship becomes holy. We *will* learn to forgive one another, we *will* learn to bless one another, and we *will* learn to release each other to our highest, most noble patterns of enlightenment and growth. The future is planned and contained in the present. What is chosen *by* us now will seem to be chosen *for* us later. The love we give is the love that will be returned to us, a thousand times over, in ways we cannot even imagine, so great is the probable light.

And similarly, whatever love we withhold—whatever we do to stop the flow of love to our door—will be reflected in our circumstances at some later date. Painful is the wheel of relationship suffering, as our romantic karma continues to haunt us until we finally let go and submit our hearts to a higher authority.

It ultimately doesn't matter what happened in the past, so much as that we take full responsibility for our part in it.

Until we do, the universe will continue to hold up a mirror to our faces: "See and, if necessary, make amends," says the mirror. Atone and forgive, that you might get off the wheel of suffering. Or don't atone, or don't forgive, and literally stay on the wheel forever.

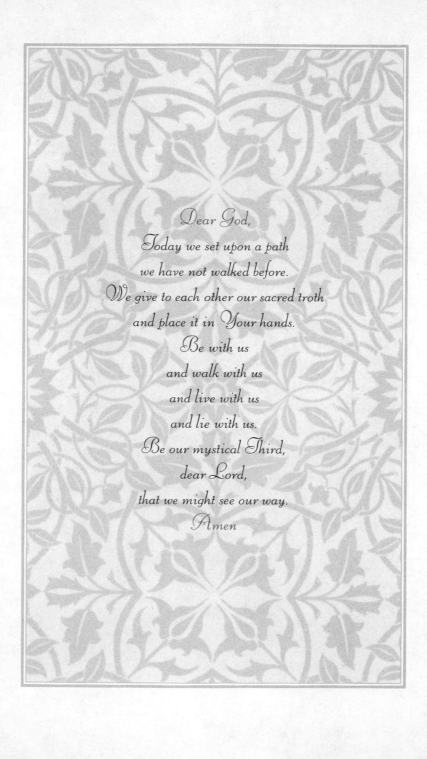

Dear God,
Today we set upon a path
we have not walked before.
We give to each other our sacred troth
and place it in Your hands.
Be with us
and walk with us
and live with us
and lie with us.
Be our mystical Third,
dear Lord,
that we might see our way.
Amen

10

_{8_

Ties That Bind

If we do this, you could imprison me.
That's true, I could try to do that.
And if you did that, I would fly away.
That, my dear, I would only assume.
If we do this, what will be in it for me?
The end to such questions,
you whispered in my ear,
Forever and ever and ever. . . .

_{8_

I ONCE ASKED an engaged couple why they were
getting married, and the woman responded to me, "Be-

cause I want to give the relationship the honor it deserves." I thought that was a pretty beautiful response. There is something about a public declaration of something that gives it deeper roots in the world around it, a gravitas it would not otherwise have. Whether or not the couple always chooses to rise to the occasion, themselves honoring the marriage through their own emotional discipline and efforts, is another story. But the environment has been created. It's easier to exercise in a room where there is gym equipment than in one where there is not.

So many energies burst forth when we love, and most of us ask ourselves at one point or another, "How far should I go? How safe is it to surrender? How deeply can I fall?" Marriage is so powerful because the response to the question becomes "All the way." There are no guarantees what will happen when you jump off an emotional cliff. You might crash on the rocks or you might develop wings. But you will never really know which one it is, until you jump.

Energy can achieve its highest manifestation only in an environment where it is allowed, totally and completely, to be what it is. That is what marriage, or any deeply committed love relationship, is at its best. It is an emotional context in which people are given complete permission to use the canvas of love to create their highest expression of themselves. One person's freedom then becomes another person's lesson in learning how not to judge. If I totally allow you the space to become the person you are capable of becoming, then the person that you might have been, that you no longer wish to be, that has to be detoxed before you can transform to your next higher level, is bound to show his or her face at times. Am I, as your partner, strong enough to stay the course and understand what's happening here, to work my own spiritual practice of nonjudgment and acceptance, not to freak out at the realization that I am stuck in a fairly small room with someone I would rather not even be in the house with?

A ring of fear surrounds love, like rings surround Saturn. But those rings are not solid, they are gaseous, and the forgiving heart flies through them as easily as an airplane flies through clouds. Once they're forgiven, they disappear. And thus the tests of love.

People are struggling today for a way to live fully and freely, unbound by conventions that no longer serve, yet within the eternal archetypes that delineate real and lasting patterns of existence. There are clearly no easy answers, but the fact that the culture is so teeming with questions is itself a very good sign. Men and women are getting to know each other at levels deeper than we knew possible, as we have begun the search for our authentic natures and, through them, the most authentic relationships. Real love and passion are indeed authentic.

Marriage, too often, is not.

Marriage is among other things very convenient, and convenience can be a very good thing. But too much convenience, too much definition, too much routine, can be the death of love. Too many marriages squeeze the love affair out of the house, and that is one of the reasons we see so many people fleeing that house as though they're running for their lives. Bills, plans, futures, money, decisions, and petty arguments are too often allowed to block the romantic view of things. Why struggle to see the depths of a person when only his or her shallow self is expected home for dinner? Enchantment begins to disappear, when life on the edge gives way to life in an eternally boring center.

The challenge for married people, then, is to not let the practicalities of life overwhelm the romance of their relationship. It takes conscious effort to protect the temple space of an enchanted love. No matter how great the marriage, no matter how much people love their spouses, there is often a sense coming from married people that an essential element of freedom is missing from their lives. Equivalent to that, of course, is a sense coming from most single people after a certain age, that an essential element of stability is missing from theirs.

Marrieds and singles are constantly sending telepathic communications to each other. There is a constant conversation everyone knows is there, but which few dare to verbalize. First, there is the silent dialogue between married and unmarried women. It is a constant unspoken discussion in which each are always saying to the other, "God, I pity you," *and,* "God, I envy you."

Unmarried women pity married women because they seem to be tied to routine, and envy them because one of the routines they can count on is his always coming home. Married women pity unmarried women because they are alone, and envy them because they seem to have opportunities for romance and adventure that married women often lack. Both women hold the key to some essential aspect of a woman's self, and it is reasonable that we all want excitement and stability both. We want inner as well as outer sustenance. Most modern relationships offer one or the other, and that is where a change is coming. We want relationships that serve the entire self.

I have seen marriages that did not seem smothered by routine. Often, however, I see an invisible prison wall around married couples, with a concomitant deadening of the eyes, resignation in the gait, and quiet though often unowned desperation. Marriage doesn't have to be a prison, of course; ultimately, it is whatever two people make of it. But I can see how much our society has invested itself in the prison model of married bliss, which is basically a model of married *guilt.* You *will* be home tonight, you *will* park your body here and here only, you *will* pour all your affection on me, you *will* deny yourself experiences that take you on a journey outside the box we live in, and you *will* pretend that this is what you really want. Most significantly, you *will* feel guilty if you find yourself feeling otherwise. And you *will* agree that I have every right to be outraged, if I find you not toeing the line.

I don't know why we're all pretending anymore; the old model of marriage is clearly not working, as evidenced by our divorce statistics. The soul is expanding to a new sense of itself, and there is no growth without freedom. We bandy the word *commitment* around as though it was uttered by God, which it was not. And if it had been, what would He have been asking us to commit to? Only to each other's bodies? I think not. I think we're being asked on this earth to commit to the revelation of Truth as it flows through our life experience. This is hardly an excuse to self-indulge or a license to do whatever feels good. Quite to the contrary, I think we should commit to the highest level of right living that we're capable of. I think we should live for others as well as ourselves. I think we should commit to the highest level of integrity we can muster. I think we should commit to taking responsibility for our own actions. I think we should commit to the effort to hear the voice for God within us, and follow its instructions to the best of our ability. And I think we should commit to the truth of a relationship as it arises organically from the relationship itself.

One of the reasons affairs are often easier than marriage is because society doesn't bother to express an opinion about what an affair should look like. On the subject of marriage, society has practically written a guidebook, an accepted set of rules basically circa 1956, which amounts to an industrial system's pronouncement not on what is good for our souls, or even our families, so much as what is good for a particular economic order. That guidebook has done as much to destroy as to build good relationships. Married people, it seems to me, should try forgetting what marriage is "supposed" to look like.

I trust freedom more than I trust rules. I think forbidden fruit is too appealing. I think the heart, when left to its own devices and honored for its own true yearnings, is good and responsible and caring of others. And I think telling other people what to do is deadly.

Married people can do the work to keep enchantment and romance alive in their marriage. But a woman who is merely living with a man can't make the man her husband, because he *isn't*. Something changes when people get married, there is certainly no doubt about that. The stakes are infinitely higher and not just for obvious reasons. A psychic shift occurs when we go through the door marked "Married"; in this extraordinarily deep rite of passage, the subtle mind is instructed to expand itself into the mind and heart of another. On an etheric level, two literally become one. On the level of our subtle bodies—made up of energy we are just beginning to scientifically understand—we can connect to another person the way an arm connects to the torso. Trying to pull an arm out of its socket would feel extraordinarily painful. Divorce can feel that bad emotionally, as any serious break-up can. But marriage is a different order of reality, a more intense connection regardless of how much love was actually shared there. For as long as people are married, there is a powerful connection through which spiritual waters flow back and forth between them, willed or not willed, conscious or unconscious.

They have entered a holy room together, whether they treat it that way or not.

Whether married or unmarried, the key to enchanted possibilities in intimacy is the element of God's love, the choice to invite a mystical Third to live with us and breathe in us. He will, if we invite Him to, consent to sit at our table and lie in our bed. There *is* a holy ghost.

The magic of love can be so hard to hold onto while we are living in this world. The veils of limitation and despair that wrap themselves around our brains each day, the obstructions to joy that are the rule and not the exception to the emotional tenor of our times, the disappointments and fears that press down on our hearts from every angle of our lives, make breaking through to a more miraculous state seem like little more than a childhood fantasy.

Yet spiritual practice makes it possible. God is always available to deliver us to the world beyond the veil. When we pray in the morning, seek prayer and meditation throughout the day, and close our eyes at night with a nod in His direction, then rays of light break through the clouds and illumine our inner skies.

What we want for our lives, and also our relationships, is to feel we are being used for something higher than our own purposes. Dear God, please use this relationship. Dear God, please use this marriage. Dear God, may innocence come forth here. Dear God, may both our souls grow stronger here. Dear God, may forgiveness be in charge here. Dear God, may we be Your servants and Your instruments, that together we might know joy.

Middle age is the age of regrets. Turning forty is hard. You are forced to take stock of your life, whether you are in the mood to do so or not.

Yet at the same time, middle age is the after party, even better than the earlier one. There is so much power that comes from attuning one's mind to what needs to be done in order to go forward. Regrets—and I know few people that are truly honest with themselves who past a certain age would say that they have none—humble us. They take us to our knees, and if we are wise, we say, "God, you and I both know that I did or did not do something I regret. Please help me atone, and help me go forward from a higher place than before." Some people regret leaving marriages that they wish now that they had never left. Others regret not going after relationships that they wish now they had pursued. Some people mourn unborn children. Some grieve various other roads taken, or not taken, that haunt them now. There is something about age that makes the seriousness of life quite obvious.

And yet people age the way wine does, when our understanding of ourselves and others is allowed to deepen and express itself fully. People we have known over the years have a value in our lives that is different than that of people we have only known a short time. There is something about two people having moved through the stages of life together, that spiritually fertilizes the garden they share. There is an ineffable depth to having walked the walk with someone, from that land called "who we used to be" to who we are today.

∽

Your hair is grayer than it used to be,
your belly softer.
I actually like this better—
You were so intimidating when you looked like God.
I couldn't see your light
through all the gold that was surrounding it.
I tripped in fear
Before your gorgeousness.
Your issues are more interesting now,

more layered and richer
In meaning and scope.
I've settled into you
Like into a comfortable chair.
Welcome to the world of the normal.
Isn't it wonderful here?

⚭

Americans and Europeans tend to take different looks at sexual fidelity, American culture more at the effect of our founding Puritans than we seem to realize. As long as Americans hang on to the notion that monogamy is the only context for a righteous romantic love, then we will be stymied in our efforts to expand to new horizons in intimacy.

I believe that God is freedom, and I believe that only in freedom is the heart honed. People don't change because there is a law, or a rule, that tells them to; we change because an experience, or wisdom, impels us to. There is a difference between sacrifice and renunciation. Sacrifice means I give something up. Renunciation means I choose willingly to let go something lower in order to achieve something higher.

A rule against something, as often as not, simply makes us

want to do it more. Monogamy has a deep and significant meaning if it results from a heartfelt desire to keep an agreement with someone we love. If the agreement stems from the belief on the part of a couple that the containment of their sexual energy to their own bond best serves their mutual growth and the growth of their relationship, then it is a holy agreement indeed. A friend of mine told me that monogamy with his wife feels like a secret password that the two of them share, to a room that only they can enter.

But if, for whatever reason, a couple chooses to hold on to certain material, emotional, or even spiritual aspects of their marriage, while perhaps letting go a monogamous agreement, then it is time for us to grow past our knee-jerk projection onto that couple that their marriage is just a sham. In fact, a marriage where two people always drag their bodies back to each other's bed, but share no significant intellectual, emotional, or spiritual connection—*that* marriage is the sham.

Monogamy in many cases has become less a soulful container for the power of sex than simply a badge of ownership. In those cases, sex can easily become more attractive with those who do *not* lay such claim on us. A rigid insistence on monogamy can actually do more to destroy than to build the connection between two people.

It's often not what we do, but the internal impetus for what we do, that establishes its significance. Agreements matter. They matter deeply. And monogamy, if from the heart, is an agreement to enter into deep communion with another human being. It can be a meaningful and very sexy gift we give to someone we love, and that we cherish as a gift from them. But to throw it around self-righteously—just one of society's leftover, no longer well-thought-out rules of behavior for a population invested in its limits to how much we will allow ourselves to love—is ridiculous and no longer worthy of who we are.

❦

WHAT IS our deepest attraction to monogamy? Our deepest attraction is not ownership but safety. While the mortal mind sees monogamy as a feast for guilt, the divine mind sees it as a feast for love. At the level of our souls, we do not want monogamy in order to imprison each other, but in order to create a context where the deepest level of safety might occur, that the deepest level of relaxation might occur, that the deepest level of growth might occur.

Some planes are simply two seaters; it's just the way they're made. There is no room in the plane for more than two people, and trying to crowd in an extra passenger could endanger the flight.

❦

If I really allow myself to love you, then a hint of madness will come over me. You have two choices. I can be totally cool all the time, or I can fall deeply, madly in love with you. Don't ask me for both. If you don't want to provide a context where I feel safe, then great, I'll stay cool. But you will probably miss the magic, which inevitably comes with risk. Only little boys say, "Show me the magic, but stay cool all the time too, will you?"

I don't mean pathological madness. That, I am absolutely responsible for. I understand that and I do the work. I am not Glenn Close and you are not Michael Douglas. No, I mean divine and righteous madness. I mean the healing crises that are induced by deep love, I mean the detoxing of the last few thousand years of dark and limited thought forms. I mean the monsters who are summoned out of their lair when the light of this love shines forth.

And that is why monogamy helps. It's enough to deal with all these monsters coming up, without also having to worry about whether

Cheryl or Sue is more attractive to you this week than I am. If you want me to really relax, and you want me to really let go and go wild, then remove those childish issues, will you?

Thank you. And I will do the same for you . . .

I didn't even take his number.

೮๑

Time can be such a threat to love. We begin to feel trapped by the illusions of the world, our limited circumstances, our withering dreams. Something about failure in any area casts a pall over every area, because it tempts us to constrict our hearts. It is painful to hope when we lack faith in ourselves. And if I look bad to myself, you start to look bad to me, too.

The beloved doesn't seem strong tonight, but weak and afraid and not the savior we had hoped for. He or she seems to have given up, and this brings up terror in both of us. We are no longer amazed; we are no longer turned on; we are no longer impressed; we feel trapped and sapped. Stress and strain and weariness and sorrow now hide from view the gossamer spring of earlier, more enchanting days. Our love was once a pastel veneer over every sky, whether blue or not, but those days are no longer with us.

We need a miracle to restore our love when guilt and sorrow have strained it. We had made of our relationship an idol, perhaps, and forgotten that only God is God. Now, as we turn back to Him, and restore our bond to the source of All, then our bond to each other is miraculously healed. We can forgive ourselves for being human, once we remember the One who is perfect, and remember that He lives in us. People falter. God does not. Accepting that is key, to both acceptance of ourselves and our acceptance of each other.

God is in love with the essence of who we are. If only we could match His mercy. . . .

⮜⮞

He got dressed this morning and left the bedroom floor a total mess.

That is not your beloved.

There are bagel crumbs all over the counter in the kitchen, and jelly on the refrigerator door.

That is not your beloved.

I am not his slave and I am tired of taking his shirts to the dry cleaners. He can take his shirts himself.

That is not your beloved.

I deserve much more than what this man is giving me.

That is not your beloved.

THEN WHO IS MY BELOVED!?

Come with me, and see . . .

❧

The only way we can see each other truly is if we see through the eyes of God.

Prayer and meditation are the fuel for the missile that takes us to enchanted realms. We spend an average of sixteen hours a day with our minds bombarded by the thinking of the world, and the thinking of the world does not glorify spirit. It glorifies personality, and in that dimension we inevitably fall short of the magnificence of enchantment. We have issues, we have weaknesses, we make mistakes, we fall short, we give up, we get caught, we fall down, we are human. And all of these make us, to the ego self, less ideal, less wonderful, less attractive.

What a trap this is for the loving heart. If love is diminished by our humanness, then what chance do we have?

The love of God is the glue that holds our hearts together when the world would pry them apart. Praying and meditating is a retreat to an enchanted castle, where we go to say,

"Time out from the world. I want to know the essential truth, the most perfect truth. I want that truth to come into me, to reveal itself to me, that I might know my love. I will stay here in this miraculous silence, and commune with my Father/Mother God. The Lord will heal me of my vicious thoughts, and give me new eyes with which to see. I will remain here in His arms for as long as it takes to repair my hurting soul. And then I will return to the world, but I will not be the same. I will have remembered who I am, and I will have remembered my precious love. I will have returned to the place of our knowing. I will have seen who he really is. I will have sought salvation in the only place where I know that I can find it. Take me back to you, dear God. Take me back to love. Amen."

Dear God,
Please show us
to each other,
and show us
how to love.
Amen

11

❧

Bodies and Soul

Over twenty years ago, I was living with my boyfriend in a fourth floor walk-up apartment in New York City. One flight above us lived a very unassuming couple. We crossed paths many times on the stairs, but they both appeared very quiet and rarely even said hello.

He was a college instructor, rather fey looking, pale and small-boned. She, also quite small, appeared as if she could fade into the woodwork. They were not, in terms most of us would relate to, a very exciting-looking couple.

And yet the noise that came through our ceiling, day in day out, from early in the morning until all hours of the night, was unbelievable. My boyfriend and I were young and in love, but our most athletic days and nights were as nothing compared to our upstairs neighbors. We would stare at each other in disbelief. *"They're doing it again!?!?!"*

In addition to the normal sounds of rocking beds and excited lovers, there was one human cry coming from their apartment over and over and over again: While we never heard a sound from him, his girlfriend ecstatically cried, *"NO!!!,"* so many times, in so many ways, with such passionate expression, that all we could do was laugh, trying to drown out their sounds by putting pillows over our ears.

It amazed me that no other word but *"No"* seemed to ever pass her lips. One night, having just heard another of her symphonies of *"No,"* I asked myself aloud, *"I wonder why she never says Yes. . . ."*

❧

THE HISTORICAL CHANGE in consciousness that defines the meaning of our age is a shift in primary focus from the body to the soul. That does not mean that the body does not matter, and it certainly does not mean that the body is bad. It simply recognizes that inner levels are causal levels, and that all outer conditions but reflect an inner state.

As the mind transforms, the body transforms. In the age now passing, the body was a house. In the age now upon us, it becomes a temple. It has housed our energies of physical survival, and is now beginning to house the energies of enlightenment. Meditation effects this change. Prayer effects this change. And when done in a consciousness of true and tender love, sex itself effects this change.

Love heals the body. Look at any woman on the day after she was made love to by a man she adores, and who adores her too. A man's body might register a difference, but a woman's body literally transforms in ways a man's does not seem to do. Our breasts, our skin, not to mention our faces, are filled with some voluptuous spirit. Both men and women walk a little bit above the sidewalk on days that follow our better nights. If there was enough happy sex in America, our crime level would be cut dramatically.

We resist joy on this planet more than we resist war. We constantly invalidate the call of our own souls, deny the song of freedom that is sung in every heart, and suppress the appreciation and adoration we truly feel for one another. Enchantment wafts over us like a wave of perfumed air, but we are afraid of its intoxicating contents. Still yet, whether we like it or not, something new is beginning to happen. We can fight it or we can breathe through it, but labor is here. The hormones of the earth are getting ready. The cervix of the as-tral human is starting to expand. The tears are beginning to fill our eyes. We are breaking free. We are breaking free. We are giving birth to something more than babies. Our true selves are being born at last.

&

IT IS A SAD COMMENTARY on our times that so many of us know more about sex than we know about love.

Magazines scream out at us constantly, "What's Sexy!" "Be Sexy!" "He or She is So Sexy!" "Sex With an Alien!" "Sex Sex Sex!"

Whoever separated God from sex should be brought up for trial, charged with emotional crimes against humanity. They took the fun out of God, making Him appear both prudish and dour—and that was just the misdemeanor! The high crime, the true spiritual felony, was taking God out of sex. We have been damaged and broken ever since.

Even when we love the most, when we have the best intentions and the true desire to do right by ourselves and others, we often find that sex can be like a bomb going off in someone's emotional life. What is it that we need to know about sex that isn't obvious on the surface?

First of all, men and women are different. We see sex differently; different hormones run through our biological systems. Nature needed different things from us, and programmed us differently to get what was needed. For millions of years, nature needed men to go from one woman to another, impregnating us as they went along in order to propagate the species. And women needed to settle down with the children, to nurture them so that they would grow into adulthood. Those impulses running through our systems for at least a few hundred thousand years turned man's instinctive response after sex into, "I gotta go," while a woman's still tends to be, "Let's settle down."

Therefore, it is incumbent upon wise men and women to take responsibility for the powerful impulses that sex brings up in all of us. Hormones are released into the body of a woman when she has had sex with a man, creating a chemical bond whether she wants that bond or not. So it is definitely not a good idea to be hooked on someone who did not consciously, benevolently, and with full responsibility ask that you be. A man's excitement in bed is great. But only a cold or foolish woman still thinks that that smile on his face when he sees that smile on yours is worth months and years of painful nights to follow. And yet that pain is bound to come, if his smile reflected the yearning of his body but not the yearning of his heart.

Most men will be pretty honest about this subject, if a woman has the nerve to ask him to be. Did the man *tell* you, "Our having sex means I will continue to call you?" Did the man *tell* you, "Our having sex means I won't be having sex with other women?" Did the man *tell* you, "Our having sex means I am entering a sacred place with you, where trying to get to know you will be a dominant factor in my life?"

Women often avoid that particular conversation. "I didn't want to ruin the magic of the moment." *Great. Now where's the magic?* "I didn't want to pressure him." *What, he can have sex with you, but he shouldn't have to answer any questions?* "He said this was only casual, but the heat was so intense that night, I thought he didn't mean it." *Darling, grow up!*

Women, and men too, often feel totally conflicted regarding the emotional responsibilities that go along with sexual encounters. Luckily, as we get older, the desperate edge which is the greatest blinder of all begins to subside and reality becomes a little clearer. Finally, conversation doesn't seem like an outrageous sacrifice, the great destroyer of a passionate moment. I laugh when I remember the days when one could never quite make it from the front door to the living room, and could only hope that the floor was clean. Now one knows how to linger over phrases, and in truth, it makes for a sexier life.

When sex isn't magical, then sex shouldn't happen. And when it is magical, its power shouldn't be underestimated. The energy exchange between two people making love is far more significant than rationalists think. That is why we can become so deeply vulnerable to someone once sex has taken place. The question is whether someone has the personality structure to contain the power of last night's behavior, the morning after and the morning after that. Will she get clingy and needy? Will he withdraw? This is where women often start getting overactive and men start wimping out. All of this is why, without some kind of commitment to the larger relationship, making love can be so emotionally risky.

೮ง

Sometimes, if we're very lucky, a hand is laid upon us which has the power, by its very touch, to claim us for its own. And once we are claimed, there is nowhere else to go. There is no man or woman or child who has quite such a silver cord wrapped around us, pulling us always in the direction of their love. Someone has put a stake on our emotional ground. We can love another but not belong to another. Once we know to whom we belong, nothing changes what we know.

It is suddenly clear that what we can learn with this one, and achieve with this one, makes every other issue pale. The alchemy between you illumines your path, leading you straight into the chamber where who you are comes up for total review and where you're going together becomes a mythical adventure. There is no blessing like being known by one who knows you this deeply. There is no mystery more alluring than this love.

We are then compelled to jump out of one orbit and into another, to make a quick run for freedom. We are compelled to use in one fell swoop the moves we have practiced for years. Every cell in our being cries out to us, "Act." Sometimes it is a sign of mastery to change major life circumstances after thinking about it for only fifteen minutes, and a sign of weakness to do anything less.

And that is because we know what we know, and we are not willing to go foggy in our lives anymore and pretend that we do not. We are not willing to hide behind the illusions of the world, the bourgeois conventions of a society which honors rules before love. We intend to go forward. We intend to take the leap of faith. We intend to grasp our love to our chest and never, ever, ever let go.

So many of us have spent years discussing the things that went wrong in love, and we have only just begun the conversation of how to do it right. The most powerful way to transform a dysfunctional past is to embrace a functional present. The most powerful way to attract great love is to fill our minds with the thought of it. The most powerful way to ensure we will be loved is if we make ourselves truly lovable.

Sometimes people are so eager to be giving in bed, but have no interest in giving anything at all when outside of bed! A prevalent neurosis in intimate relationships is how loath many people are to give anything up. A narcissistic generation grew up with the attitude, "I have my wants, desires, needs, habits and predilections. *I have no intention of giving any of them up to be with you.*"

When love's enchantment is of interest to us, then doing something, or not doing something, for no other reason than that it pleases our partner, is hardly seen as failure to be authentically oneself, but rather mastery at the art of love.

A couple came to one of my groups saying they had a problem. Melissa, said George, was a "touchy-feely" sort of woman, disposed toward light, affectionate physical contact with whomever she was speaking to. According to George, however, she displayed this affection with other men in a way that he felt went over the line, from platonic affection to sexual flirtatiousness. I asked Melissa for her take on this. She described a situation where she had touched a mutual friend of theirs, and George hadn't liked it. "But I'm not even conscious of it when I'm doing it!" she exclaimed.

I asked George to describe that moment.

"She didn't just touch him," he said. "She stroked his neck and that kind of thing."

I looked at Melissa. She didn't argue.

"How would you be with it if she hugged people, even men, upon seeing them?" I asked him.

"That would be fine with me," he said. "I don't care about that. It's when there's this sexual edge to it that I mind."

"Is that true?" I asked her. "Is there a sexual edge to it when you flirt with men in front of him?"

Once again, she said nothing.

"Melissa," I said. "Do you want George to remain attracted to you?"

"Yes," she replied.

"Do you want him to feel good about himself in your presence? Do you want him to find being with you exciting and fun? Do you want him to keep wanting you?"

"Yes."

"Then, Melissa," I said. *"Cut it out."*

They both laughed, and they both looked relieved.

What Melissa was just learning was a very important key to intimacy: *Some things you do for no other reason than that it makes another person feel good.* I grew up in a generation so clueless on these subjects as to think thoughts like, "It's not my responsibility to make you happy." Now I think, "No, it's not my responsibility—but it sure is a good idea!"

If George had been asking Melissa to compromise her own integrity, standards, or goals in life, then that would be a completely different story, of course. But there is a very big difference between substantial issues—which should never be compromised—and surface issues, our flexibility with which can make all the difference to another person's happiness.

It's a matter of deciding what you want. Both George and Melissa had already agreed that Melissa did not like to see other women hitting on George in *her* presence. I told Melissa that if she would make this change—if George saw her consciously and willingly refraining from touching other men in his presence—that I bet he would more than make up for any sacrifice she thought she had made for him, later that night. She knew, of course, and he knew, that I was right.

ANOTHER COUPLE told a story with similar implications. His name is Brian, hers is Suzanne.

"I had a free airline ticket to anywhere in the country," he said, "but only a thirty-day window to use it. My wife couldn't get off from work during that time, and she agreed I should go somewhere.

"So where I wanted to go was to Hawaii. She said that was the one place she didn't want me to go, because she thought it was so romantic and she had always wanted us to go there together.

"I couldn't understand why I shouldn't go there now, and then we'd go there again, together, at a later time. I promised her we would. But she kept saying that it really hurt her feelings that I would go there. I thought that made no sense, so I went there anyway. Now I'm back, but I can feel the energy between us isn't the same."

I asked Suzanne how she saw the situation. She said that Brian's version of the story was correct. It really hurt her that he didn't honor her feelings about this, however irrational they might have seemed to him.

I understood Suzanne's point. I told Brian that a woman's feelings aren't necessarily *rational;* they're just *feelings.* But there's little more exciting energy in the universe than the energy of a woman when she is truly happy. This wasn't about who is right—there is no *right* here. What there is, is a question: Is your partner just your friend, someone walking through life on a parallel track, or is your partner someone with whom you are connected in an ever more intricately woven tapestry of mutual giving, sharing, and delight? The only reason for Brian not to have gone to Hawaii on this trip would have been in order to reap the highest possible emotional advantages from his marriage. Hawaii has external blessings, to be sure, but he chose to risk some internal blessings by going there at this time. He missed an opportunity that he might, given another, more romantic perspective, have jumped at: the chance to make his wife happy.

A few moments passed. Then Brian looked at Suzanne and said, "I'm sorry."

The whole room melted. I even saw a few tears.

BRIAN IS A MAN who is learning to cherish a woman's feelings. Just as important is that a woman learn to respect a man's thoughts.

"My problem is my husband," Kate said.

That alone—the expression, "My problem is my husband"—said a lot.

"He's a wonderful man, and a wonderful father to our three-year-old little boy. I love my husband very much. But he has become an agnostic. He used to be very religious and then he started reading all about other religions and metaphysics and all, and now he says he doesn't know what he believes."

She stopped speaking.

"Forgive me," I said. "I don't see the problem."

"Well it's about my little boy," she continued. "I'm so worried what effect this will have on him, that his father doesn't know whether he believes in God or not!"

I said to her, "If you're interested in your son's psychological and spiritual development, then the best thing you can do is teach him to respect his father. That very much includes his father's intellectual journey. Your husband is undertaking a difficult but courageous task; he's actually thinking for himself. You should be proud of that and respect it. It's the journey of his mind, and this particular kind of questioning is part of the journey of his generation.

"To show respect for your husband's thoughts, particularly when they're so obviously serious, is the greatest gift you can give to yourself, your marriage, your husband and your son. You don't have to agree with someone's intellectual conclusion to respect the journey that led them to it. Notice the insidious ways that the ego mind will always tempt us to judge another person, particularly those we love the most, and try to use that love as justification for our judgment.

"The problem as you describe it is not about God. It's about respecting a man, and teaching his children to respect him, too. And *that*, in fact, *is* about God."

She got it. In fact, they both sent me flowers. . . .

ॐ

SO THE ISSUE of intimacy is one issue only: Relationship means joining, and joining is not of the body—joining is of the spirit. Every problem in the world, from war to domestic violence, is a result of hearts being separate. Anytime, anywhere, when two hearts join, the world is brought a little closer to heaven. But hell is embedded in our thought system here. Even in our most intimate relationships, we're invested in finding guilt, and often we use sex as a means of closing the emotional gap that the guilt produced. We are learning now that the only level of true healing is the level of the heart.

When sex is merely a substitute for communication, or even worse, an expression of anger, then of course it heals nothing. When it deepens conversation, because words alone cannot possibly express the feelings that maybe, just maybe, my hand caressing your face could express, then the body is being used to serve something higher than the body. Love itself, not the body itself, is the healer of all things.

It does bear noting, of course, that knowing this only makes sex better. The body takes us beyond the body. Then it becomes a door to a realm that the body can't even enter.

Dear God,
I have lost my love.
I feel as though my heart is broken
and will never repair.
Please help me, God,
get over this.
Reveal to me the truth,
and show me
a love that never dies.
Amen

12

&

When Form Changes

A friend of mine used to e-mail me almost every day. One morning I received an e-mail from him that read, "Same message: eternally grateful we ended up in the same town at the same time."

There was another e-mail he sent that day, but it was fairly mundane. I didn't even remember what it was.

Hours after he wrote those notes, having flown across the country, my friend dropped dead of a heart attack. We never had a chance to say good-bye.

Later that day I said to my secretary, "Please print out those last e-mails from Andrew. I want to save them now."

That night, I had a dream. In it, the phone rang and I

answered it casually. "It's Andrew," said the voice at the other end of the line. I saw him sitting in a chair, speaking into the phone.

While his only words were "It's Andrew," I got the sense in the dream that he been given some kind of special permission to make this call to me.

I was totally freaked by this dream. I awoke suddenly from my sleep, sat up quickly in bed, and cried out "Oh my God . . . !" I felt absolutely that I had been contacted by the dead.

The next day, or perhaps the day after, I was sitting at my desk, speaking on the phone and thumbing through files. I saw the one marked "Andrew's last e-mails" that my secretary had prepared. Opening it, I saw his two last notes to me: the second one—the one I had thought said nothing important—read, "Wherever I am tonight, I'll try to call you."

⌘

WHEN RELATIONSHIPS are "over," they're not really over. The body is just an encasement for the spirit of love, and whether bodies come or go—even whether they are physically alive or not—is not what determines the existence of love, its substantiality or its eternal significance.

All things that exist in truth exist forever. Birth doesn't begin our existence and death doesn't end it. And the same holds true for relationships. Whom God hath brought together cannot be torn assunder, not really. Once we've bonded with someone in the spirit of true love, then we can relax and just know that this love is ours forever. Your beloved can move to China, divorce you and marry someone else, or even say he or she hates you, but the real truth stays true for all time. What is love is eternal. No one's opinion or momentary emotions can change this. Relationships last forever, and love can never die.

If you've still got healing to do with someone, then it might take five days or it might take five thousand years, but you will be coming together again for the chance to make that happen. Otherwise the will of God will not be done, and the will of God cannot not happen. The union of souls is the will of God, and the entire universe is invested in His plan. Anytime there's conflict between anyone, for any reason, the harmony of God's universe is disrupted. Divine spirit is like an ubiquitous, all-powerful bio-computer, leading everyone to the people and circumstances that provide the maximal opportunities to learn the lessons of love and forgiveness. That is the overriding drama of life on earth. We will someday be rejoined—all of us with all of us—and the rapture of that reunion will light up the world.

Anytime two hearts join, anytime any of us reach beyond the walls that separate us, the entire world moves closer to heaven. One link in a broken chain has been restored, and the formerly disconnected links are even stronger than before. The chain of the Atonement links all of us together and to God.

Disconnection between us can be so painful. The struggle most lovers live through, on some level, is the harmonizing between our soul purpose, i.e. our desire to connect, and our earth purpose, i.e. our need to individuate. Finding a way to integrate the two is the basic challenge of a spiritually mature love.

Many of us have loved people whose sense of relationship was more fluid, less form-based, more "Let's not define it, let's just see what it is" than ours. Other times, *we're* the voice that sounds more like that, compared to someone else! We're living at a time when old thought forms often do not apply, and we are struggling to find the perfect balance between freedom and responsibility. Creating the right vessel for love can be a challenge, indeed: Where are we allowing form to smother our love, and where are we using form to merely give it structure, making it more meaningful in the physical world? Too much focus on form, and the love itself—the needs of the people themselves—can seem left out of the equation. But if all we do is embrace a free-form love, valuing freedom and independence over responsibilities and commitments, then it's as though we're just embracing the wind. The answer here is to hold form, but to hold it lightly, like a very simple frame around a beautiful picture.

Somewhere there is a golden mean, where yes, we are free, and yes, we have earthly responsibilities as well. Yes, you get to feel whatever you feel for whomever you feel it for, and yes, there are principles of integrity here that matter as well, and promises, and people who have a right to feel that your word means something very meaningful and substantial. If all someone's love means is "I feel for you, and that will never change," then great, but that we can get from a dead person! We took on bodies for a reason. Love is not something to merely feel. It is something to be chosen, to make a stand for, to lay claim to, to incarnate fully. Otherwise there is a waste on some level of our precious time on earth.

Boundaries in love are like building codes in construction. They're a pain to adhere to sometimes, but without them, things can get dangerous later on. And when integrity and righteousness are adhered to and demanded, then they do not kill love but rather lift it to a higher place. We don't ever have to worry that a psychologically more sound existence will destroy the romance of life; at the highest level, spiritual and psychological truth are one. They need each other, for each, if unbalanced by the other, can deteriorate into half-truths. They are the yin and yang of all relationships, including intimate ones. Yes, I want to love you at night, but I also want to like you during the day. Yes, I want to fly through the sky with you, but I also want to stroll with you down Main Street. A grown-up at love knows how to do both, and doesn't try to sacrifice one for the other.

I have felt before, "Oh, this is so disappointing. I'm starting to see what his real psychological issues are, and he's starting to see mine. There goes the romance! So much for the ideal!" But in fact, that's not when romance dies. It's simply when illusions die. Disillusionment, after all, implies you were laboring under illusions in the first place! The moment that our real "issues" are exposed is simply when two people have the opportunity to go deeper, to explore further, to heal faster, to communicate more sincerely, to be more honest, and to love more truly. Yes, for a few minutes it will seem as though someone turned the music off and blew out the candles, but if the partners hold to the highest pursuit of both integrity and forgiveness at this moment of truth, then the water will indeed be crossed, the music will come on again, the candles will be relit, and the romance will become even deeper and more passionate. But you will only get to find that out if you have the guts to stay the course. Otherwise, you just jump from pink to more pink, when you could have had an entire rainbow.

❧

I don't know what to do with this storm. Large gray clouds, cold winds, choppy waters in the ocean beneath this cliff—all of them fill my heart. I am standing in a long red dress and bonnet, peering across the horizon, and I am looking . . . for what? Is your ship even out there? Is it on the sea at all?

My mind lacks information, and in this state of indefinition and perplexity, I long for calm. I return to the house. I drink tea and then I close my eyes. I am supported by the knowledge that I know you love me, and the choppy sea is yours, not mine.

❧

And then, of course, there are times when it is really over. Not spiritually, as we have already seen, but in the realm of this earthly existence. Yes, he will stay in your heart forever, and you will stay in his. But there will be no more midnight conversations, morning kisses, or children crawling into bed with you. One of you, or both of you, said "No" . . . and so it is.

Perhaps there was wisdom in that decision, and perhaps there was not. Either way, one or both of you will probably cry. Either the spirit of God led you on to better things, or the gift of this love was too great for someone invested in their limits to endure. It doesn't matter, on a certain level. The grief is still the same.

And yet the grief itself has a way of honing us and shaping us. It softens us and humbles us. And then we are more prepared for love. There is no reason to grow bitter when love departs. No one wronged you so much as they might have wronged themselves. And I do believe the statement that nature abhors a vacuum. For every tear in anyone's eye, there is someone out there to kiss it away.

Whether the path of life or the mystery of death has taken our true love from us, we learn something very important from the experience: God, and God alone, never leaves. He was there, is there, and will always be there. He lifts us above the hellish darkness that can sink our hearts and rob us of our joy. Our emotions need not be battered by the winds of fate, for God himself would have us walk on water. He literally lifts our spirits, and we come to know that we are safe to love, we are safe to be vulnerable, and we are safe to surrender—not because the beloved will necessarily remain here always, but because we know we will be fine in the arms of God, even if he does not.

⁊

WE CAN'T MAKE CHOICES for another person. However clearly we might think we see the light of infinite possibility, if our beloved sees no possibility at all, then that is his or her choice. We need to let go of the physical habits we have associated with this love, that is true, but we never, ever have to let go of the love itself. It remains with us because it is part of God. It will be part of us until the day we die, and I assume it will be part of us forever after that.

To forgive a love is to let go the things of the body, and embrace fully the things of spirit. Spirit can never be diminished or sacrificed in any way. Every love is part of every other love, and every love builds on the love that came before. Love is a mighty trajectory, moving through our lives by divine design, appearing to be composed of separate loves, yet that is just illusion. Like stars in the distant sky appearing to twinkle on and off, it might seem that we are "in" a relationship, and at another time we are "out" of relationship, but such is just a silly story that has no meaning in heaven. We are always in love, for love is always in us. Different smiles and different faces mean nothing. There is only one love. There is only one love.

I set you up to leave, of course. I see that now. People used to say to me, "Don't you think you deserve love?" But I couldn't see how to relate to that question. Now I see that for every time that I have cut off love, someone has cut off their love from me. Not because God has punished me, but because I have punished myself. Guilt demands punishment, and subconsciously I felt guilty. I programmed you to punish me. I see that now, and I free us both. Thanks for playing your part so well. I wish for you, and I wish for me, a happier drama, a kinder end, and a sweeter ride than the one we put each other through.

Someday, when all of this is over, we will laugh at this. And you

will say, "Do you remember when you were so mad at me, when I
wanted to take that trip with my friends?"

And I will say, "Yes, I remember that. I didn't know it, of course,
but I was totally invested in making you a monster, and I couldn't
think of any other way to do it."

"You did quite well," you will say to me.

"But hallelujah," I will say to myself. "I don't have to do that
anymore—to you or to me or to anyone."

ॐ

WITH HALF of all American marriages ending in divorce,
we desperately need to embrace a more sacred way of dealing
with this experience. We need it for ourselves, and most im-
portantly, we need it for our children.

Divorce is not necessarily a real end. It is a change, to be sure,
and an end to one form of a relationship—but it need not be
an end to what is most important. If you have children with
someone, then they are your family. And that family remains.
Most divorced people I know would want very much to find a
way to have a friendly, loving relationship with their ex, if they
only knew how. And those who do are so clearly blessed.

In my book *Illuminata*, I wrote a sacred "divorce ceremony" that prayerfully guides a couple to place their now-ending marriage in the hands of God. It blesses the bond that does not die and surrenders the one that does. God is asked to illumine the transition. What violence is wrought, in our hearts and in our children's hearts, when there is no grace around something this painful and significant.

Whether or not we choose to participate in such a ceremony, the murmuring of our hearts can still secure the blessings of the Lord.

❧

Dear God,
We place this marriage
and this divorce
in Your hands.
Heal our hearts, dear God,
and heal our children.
We release each other in love,
and we bless each other forever.
Help us to forgive the past,
to see the beauty and innocence

in ourselves
and each other.
We thank each other for the good times,
and forgive each other for everything else.
May nothing in the past
except its blessing
remain with either one of us.
We thank each other
for the many gifts,
and vow to hold them in our hearts forever.
In this moment,
may our relationship be reborn,
to serve this new season of our lives.
May the Holy Spirit
guide us and bless us.
Forgive us both,
dear God.
Amen.

ᕆᕐ

And when our beloved has passed from physical existence,
a chapter in our relationship with that person is over. But the

book of life itself never ends. If our beloved dies, he or she will be as an angel on our shoulder. And if our hearts are open, we will feel their wings brush gently up against our neck, every time we turn around.

ↄ

Dear God,
Please tie a golden cord,
one end to my beloved's heart
and one end to mine.
With Your hand upon this cord, dear God,
please make our bond eternal.
May neither sickness nor pain,
conflict nor death,
defeat or take away our love.
Cement my heart
to the heart of my beloved,
forever and ever.
Amen.

ↄ

If the person we love still lives, but has withdrawn his or her affection, then it is possible that cords of energy still connect us in unhealthy ways. At such a time, it is best to ask God to remove those cords, to even cauterize their ends, that we might be free of attachments that no longer serve. Through sex and longing and depth of emotion, we can find ourselves tied to places and situations no longer useful to our journey. Then it is time to cry, and to pray, and to deepen. Yet such moments help inform us of the nature of love, and thus the nature of life. We come to understand more deeply who we really are and why we came here. When we see that, we begin to smile again.

And in time, we will begin to laugh.

Dear God,
Receive my praise
and thanksgiving
for the love
that is in my arms.
Amen

13

❧

Song of the Beloved

On the day when you said yes, I sat down and could not believe my search was over. Yes, there will be no more emotional back alleys, where I have wandered in the hopes of being fed. Yes, now I had better put up, after all my protestations that I'm the one for you. Yes, it is true, the holiness and power in the air tonight mean I have ended one life and begun another.

No, I do not feel confident that I will not trip or fall. No, I do not always feel good enough to be at your side. No, I do not feel absolutely sure of the decision we have made. But neither do I feel I have a choice. For my heart calls out from an ancient place and declares you are the one—that to be with you and walk with you and pray with you and cry with you will hone my soul and redeem my past, and free my song at last. When it does, I will sing for you. And then we shall both be free.

Come with me now, into a forest deep. I will not let go your hand. There is waiting there, in a grove of grass, a surprise that will make you laugh. You will feel there like a child again, and we will play among the wild. I will not be who you see before you, yet you will recognize my eyes. Lion, tiger, lamb and bird, I will magnify your every thought and be your every dream. Pet and lover, mother, sister, queen and servant shall I be, until you rise from all still dreaming to be alive at last. And when you do, I only hope that I will still be yours. I do not take for granted this, but wish with all my heart. Your light this day relieves my heart; your light that day will penetrate the darkness of my pain. Then I will rise like the phoenix bird and join with you in flight. We will not be who we used to be. We will be angels then.

I will fly, if you will fly. We will fly as one. We will not regret the choice we made, to love each other now. For we both know the pain we knew, walking the corridors of a loveless world. We will hold each other up. We will free each other's soul to sing. The music of the universe will reconstruct our souls. The love we share will light the sky, and dark shall be no more. God will surely join us there. Hallelujah, we shall sing, and fall into His arms. Fall into mine for now, my love, and I will make you glad.

This is the day the Lord hath made, this is the table prepared for us, this is the love to heal us both. Thank you God, for my love at my side. Thank you God, for everything. Thank you God, for all of this. Thank you God, for you.

℘

THE HEART BECOMES supple, or love cannot find us. Walls cannot join with one another, but tender spirits can. And in that joining, a power greater than the sum of its parts is released into the universe. A mysterious laser enters into us, expanding who we are, altering our personal boundary lines, redesigning the map of our former existence. We are becoming who we need to be to stand at each other's side.

And thus is created the space called "we"—not you, not me, but a sacred dimension called "we." A space to be honored, protected, and, above all, cherished. A space of love that is not of this world, but with the power to transform it. It is a hospital for the broken spirits of the two who have arrived here, a place to rest after years at war, and a womb for the preparation of the identities we are forging now. We were born alone, but we will be reborn as cosmic twins.

And that is what we find, when we finally ascend to the highest peaks of love. Enchanted intimacy bestows a shared ministry, a common mission of two souls in service to a force that is bigger than either one. We are separate and we are one as well—indeed, as is all humanity. It is time to live as if our oneness mattered. We seek, through an enchanted love, to live the principles we so fervently wish to see guide our civilization. They are the principles that already guide the stars, and naturally guide the hearts of those who are in love. That is why lovers are the natural leaders of the dawning age. Enchantment restores our better nature. Both of us feel, "What I want, more than anything, is to be my best for you. What I want, more than anything, is to provide you with warmth in all the places where you have wandered in the cold for so long. What I want is to become someone who gives to you with the naturalness of a fountain giving water, and receives from you with the graciousness with which the earth receives the rain."

Allow your mind to gently embrace the image of your beloved. Now see, with your mind's eye, an angelic presence, a being of light who stands at his or her side. Allow yourself to slip into the luminous skin of this angelic force, to merge with its light and then to gently become it. Ask God to make you a profound beneficence in the life of the one you love.

Pray that the doors to love be opened in your heart. Dear God, please make me a giver, not a taker. Dear God, please make this love a playground for our higher selves. Dear God, please make my beloved a very happy person. Dear God, please use me to restore her smile, to repair his heart, to promote the healing of my lover's life. And with our love and through our love, dear God, please heal the world. I vow to try to do my best. Please bless us both. Amen.

☙

There is such stillness here in this place, where there is only you and I, with the knowledge that this has been going on forever. We paused in conversation, for what—a thousand years? Speak to me again, for your voice is coded with the music I have longed to hear. I will join you in this dialogue, I will speak my word and sing my part. The silence lasted long enough, and it is time to begin again.

Say yes, and you will never be sorry. Say yes, say yes, say yes, say yes . . .

☙

ALL JOINING of hearts is a joining in God; there is no love but God's. Each love we share is a facet of His Light, in a cosmic diamond as real as anything we can see or feel in the physical world.

Enchantment builds a bridge across time and space, compensating for whatever apparent lack there is in our normal modes of communication. If I'm one with you in the realm of enchantment, yet lack either phone or emotional permission to call, you might just happen to hear a song on the radio that says to you what I would say if I were at your side.

The song was not played "by accident," and you know it. You feel it. This is the kind of thing that occurs naturally in the presence of love. It is part of a mystical fabric that is woven between those who love and claim enchantment. Our old, mechanistic modes of being are like old airplanes next to the space shuttle, compared to the illumined capacities that spring forth when our hearts are open. These new capacities are not metaphorical; they are very real. They include the ability to fly across time and space (when we love each other enough, we will not need airplanes), communicate across time and space (when we love each other enough, we will no longer need the Internet), and bring peace to all the world (when we love each other enough, we will have no need for war).

Enchanted lovers create a hole in the wall now blocking our view of paradise. The wall will come down in the world, when it crumbles in our hearts.

෬

So this is the adventure I propose to you: I want every thought and every feeling, every hope and every dream, every fear and every pain. I want them all. I will put them in my pot and pour in spices from the East. I will stir them with my will, and add my love and prayers for you. Later you will dine with me, and the food you eat will make you strong. Your shallow self will cook away, into the depth you carry in you. Bring to me your hunger, and I will feed you from my womanself.

Bring to me your yearning, for I am big enough to meet you there. I bring with me a spirit who will dwell with us forever. It will make of our love an enchanted place, and we will become who we are.

Now come up to the wall with me, and the wall will disappear, my love.

The wall will disappear.

෬

Acknowledgments

Thanks to Al Lowman and Mitchell Ivers for being my midwives on this book. Thanks to Simon & Schuster for allowing me the privilege of publishing it. Thanks to Anne-Marie Wilk, Kathy Kalil, and Mary Ellen Bushy for making my world work while I was writing it. And thank you to Emma for making Mommy's heart so very glad.

About the Author

Marianne Williamson has been lecturing on meta-physics and spirituality since 1983. She is the best-selling author of *A Return to Love*, *A Woman's Worth*, *Illuminata*, *Emma and Mommy Talk to God*, and *Healing the Soul of America*, a revised and expanded version of *The Healing of America*. She is the spiritual leader of the Church of Today in Warren, Michigan.